THRIVING
THROUGH
YOUR
STORMS

Thriving Through Your Storms:
12 Profound Lessons to Help You Grow Through
Anything You Go Through in Life

Published by

Platinum Performance Global, LLC.

ISBN: 978-0-9721324-1-1

To order copies of this book in bulk for book clubs, community meetings,
company staff, professional association membership, church study groups,
employee moral & reward programs or non-profit fundraisers, please visit or call
(813) 963-5356 for special pricing.

Editing and book design by Stacey Aaronson
Transcription by Dana Visak
Cover design by Nisha

Printed in the United States of America

Thriving Through Your Storms

12 Profound Lessons to Help You Grow Through Anything You Go Through in Life

Delatorro L. McNeal, II

Platinum Performance Global, LLC

Other Books
by Delatorro McNeal, II

....

Caught Between a Dream and a Job:
How to Leave the 9-to-5 Behind and
Step into the Life You've Always Wanted

The Rules of the Game:
How to Write Your Own Ticket in College and Beyond

101 Gems of Greatness

Audio/Video Training & Coaching Programs
by Delatorro McNeal, II

....

Thriving Through Your Storms
5-Disc Audio Coaching Program

Caught Between a Dream and a Job
10-Disc Mega Coaching Success System

The Full Throttle Experience
12-DVD Live Conference

Presenting Your Way to Greatness
12-Disc Speaking and Communication Mastery System

I dedicate this book to everyone who has, is, or will be going through the storms of life. It is my sincere hope, prayer, and expectation that you will utilize this book to help you learn how to THRIVE Through Your Storms and help others do the same.

Life is not about waiting for the storm to pass,
it's about learning how to dance in the rain.

—Anonymous

Claim your free 5-part video series ($197 value)
to accompany this book by visiting
www.thrivingthroughyourstorms.com

TABLE OF CONTENTS

PART ONE
The Psychology of Adversity

PART TWO
The Components of Your Comeback

Introduction

"Don't you ever let the people, the problems, and the pain of your past pause your present, punish your person, imprison your potential, and paralyze your progress."

Empowered greetings, my friend. Wherever you're reading this book—whether it's at home or in your office, at the park, the beach, the airport, or on an airplane, boat, or train—I'm right there with you as you absorb this information that is literally going to transform your life.

I want you to understand something: Pain is not prejudice. All of us have to go through challenging and difficult times, and storms come in all forms:

+ Relationships
+ Careers
+ Socioeconomic statuses
+ Academic levels
+ Neighborhoods

+ Families
+ Faiths
+ Businesses
+ Physical health
+ Emotional states

Pain and adversity affect everybody, and when there's a change in the tide, it affects big and small ships alike, whether you're on Wall Street or Main Street, in the upper, middle, or lower class. This book was designed to strategically, systematically, and instructionally help you overcome, win, and succeed in the midst of any situation you're going through. I'm excited and delighted to welcome you to *Thriving Through Your Storms*.

My friend, I want you to understand that it's not *what* you go through, it's *how* you go through it. That's why this book is titled *Thriving Through Your Storms*, because I don't want you to just survive—that's reactive. I want you to thrive—that's proactive.

Personally, I've never had the luxury of stopping in the middle of a storm. When difficult times have hit my life (which they have from the time I was born), I've never been able to sit out for a year; I've always had to keep going. So although I have a résumé of accomplishments and accolades that come behind my name, all of them have been earned through failure. And I imagine all of yours have as well.

In the following chapters, we're going to learn how to find what Iyanla Vanzant calls "value in the valley," which relates to what the Scriptures call "the lily in the valley." Together, we're going to learn how to find the sunshine in the midst of the rain that's going on in your life, that silver lining in the cloud of doubt that seems to be looming over your head with regard to your business, marriage, health, friendships, and finances. No matter what it is, my friend, I want you to understand that I'm here to help you make it through it. And you're not getting ready to learn from someone who's had nothing but success all his life. I know what it's like to:

✦ be labeled at-risk when I was in grade school
✦ have sick parents in my adult life
✦ go through divorce
✦ experience public embarrassment
✦ lose my mother
✦ be fired from a corporate job
✦ have a house foreclosed on
✦ lose valuable friendships
✦ be faced with health problems
✦ deal with business challenges in the middle of a recession

But in spite of all those challenging times, I also know what it's like to learn how to thrive in the midst of them. And what I want you to understand is that pain and adversity have no pedigree. They don't discriminate; they know where to find us. So we have to learn how to thrive in the midst of our storms.

When you're going through tough times, there are a lot of things you cannot control. This book is designed to help you gain control, especially when it comes to your attitude and mindset toward what you're going through. Anthony Robbins says that success and adversity are both 80% psychology and 20% mechanics. And that's what these chapters are about —helping you develop the mindset and methodology to thrive through challenging times. As a result of this learning, you might be inspired to seek professional help if you need additional support. I often see people go through train wrecks in their life, and they try to walk away without ever getting professional help. My friend, there are folks out there who would love to coach you through your difficult times. Don't be so proud that you can't reach out to them.

> Your problem is not your problem. It's the way you're thinking about your problem that's the problem.

One of the biggest things I hope this book does for you is change your neurological association to the purpose and/or meaning of the pain you're experiencing in your life right now. In short, I hope this book helps you develop new, powerful, and helpful *meanings* regarding your storms. You see, my friend, I learned something very profound a long time ago while listening to my mentor, Anthony Robbins. He said:

"Nothing has any meaning absent of the meaning we associate to it."

One of the biggest things I've realized we do to prolong our own storms in life is attach and associate a ton of negative to the things that happen to us

—toxic purposes and meanings to our pain that make us do the following in our storms:

✦ Stay

✦ Stew

✦ Become addicts

✦ Develop bad habits

✦ Retreat

✦ Get depressed

✦ Get mad at God

✦ Hurt the people we love

✦ Self-medicate

✦ Mask tremendous pain

rather than learn to:

✦ Thrive Through Our Storms

That's what this book is about ... Learning how to THRIVE!

But in order to do so, you have to change the *meaning* you associate with the things that happen to you. Because as long as you connect negative meanings to them, you can never be free, and you can never thrive. But the moment you're willing to replace negative and unproductive meanings with positive and productive ones, *everything* changes in your favor, my friend. Everything!

You see, the moment you attach meaning to something, you create a mathematical equation in your own mind.

✦ This = That

   as in ...

✦ My Storms = Failure

✦ My Storms = God's mad at me

✦ My Storms = I'm not good enough

✦ My Storms = I'm a bad parent

✦ My Storms = Nobody will ever love me again

✦ My Storms = I will never get back on top financially

✦ My Storms = Fill in the blank _____

Get my point?

As long as you associate a negative meaning to your storms, you can never, ever thrive; the game is over before you even start. However, when you change the meaning, you change the equation too.

✦ My Storms = New opportunities for me
✦ My Storms = New beginnings for me
✦ My Storms = A chance for me to grow
✦ My Storms = Getting rid of my unnecessary relationships
✦ My Storms = New focus and direction for my life
✦ My Storms = Seeing what I'm really made of

The storms that come into our lives are trying to teach us something and help us grow, so it's vital to learn to look at them in that way.

Up to this point, you may have been using the wrong equations in your mind. Equations like:

✦ My Failed Business = People don't care about my dream
✦ My Bad Credit = I will always pay high interest
✦ My Layoff = I'll be broke for the next two years
✦ My Diagnosis = I'll be sick the rest of my life
✦ My Divorce = No one will ever love me again
✦ My Debt = I'll never be financially free
✦ My Jealous Friends = I'll never have people who support my dreams
✦ My Abusive Childhood = People will always take advantage of me
✦ My Low Self-Esteem = I'll never live a fulfilling/confident life

My friend, *all* of these meanings we effortlessly attach to the storms we face in life are all 100% garbage! What's worse, they're all a big, fat lie.

In order to change the negative association/meaning you attach to what happens in your life, you have to change the mental/mathematical equation you use. How?

Here's a much better equation to begin using right now that will show you exactly how to pull a positive and productive meaning out of any storm you face or have faced:

$$E + R = O$$

Event + Response = Outcome

My good friend and globally respected bestselling author, entrepreneur, and speaker Jack Canfield taught me this. By adopting this one new equation into your daily belief system, you will change the way you process everything that happens to you—good or bad!

You see, the natural equation most people embrace is that the Event that happened to you is automatically equated to the Outcome. But you're no longer one of those people! You now realize that the Event + your Response to the event = the Outcome.

So if the event is negative but you create a positive *response* to that event, the end result is always positive!

Let's look at an illustration where we assign a number to the elements:

> Event (you got laid off) **-10**
>
> +
>
> Response (you find a better career) **50**
>
> =
>
> Outcome (you're 10 times happier and more
> fulfilled with your work) **40**

See how that works?

It's the *response* or the *meaning* you associate to the Event that determines the end result and the overall Outcome.

So welcome to this amazing work that will challenge *how you respond* to the storms that come into your life. It will also challenge the way you have responded to storms in your past, showing you better ways to process them so you can move forward even more powerfully than before. Lastly, as a direct result of this book, you will handle *future* storms in a way that will empower you to *thrive* right in the middle of what you're going through.

Let's get down to the business of changing your life!

I'm ready ... are you? Because the next 12 chapters are going to rock your world!

Your Platinum Partner,

Delatorro L. McNeal, II

Delatorro L. McNeal, II, MS, CSP

PART ONE

The Psychology of Adversity

You
Must
Be
Prepared

1

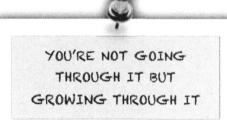

YOU'RE NOT GOING
THROUGH IT BUT
GROWING THROUGH IT

I'll never forget one Sunday in church when a guest pastor came and spoke. He said something brief but powerful, not only in *what* he said but in *how* he said it, and I've never been able to shake it.

This well-known pastor was Bishop Noel Jones, and his statement moved me to write this chapter. He said: "What you cannot avoid you must be prepared for." When I heard that it set something off in me, and I began to think about us dealing with our storms—our difficulties, challenges, and issues in life.

The reality is, as I've already shared with you, there's no way we're going to get out of this thing called life without trouble, adversity, hardship, and trials. But the key—and this is vital if you're going to thrive through your storms—is to understand that what you cannot avoid, you must be prepared for. You may have heard this before, but you may not have realized that at any given time, you're in one of three places in life:

> 1. You're in a storm
> 2. You're heading toward a storm
> 3. You just left a storm

What this means, my friend, is that at the end of the day, we need to learn how to thrive through our storms, and in order to do so, we must adopt a new mindset that says this: What I cannot avoid, I must be prepared for.

Think about this example: If you anticipate that it's going to rain, what do you do?

+ You wear appropriate clothes.
+ You take an umbrella.
+ You put on the right shoes.
+ You plan differently.

Because it's raining, you may need to adjust your schedule, but you still go out and do whatever it is you need to do; you drive with more focus and caution, paying closer attention to other drivers. Then once you get to your destination, you don't just stroll up to the store, the mall, the bank, wherever you're going—you beeline to it to get out of the rain, right?

The point is that you can't avoid challenges and difficult situations in life. Sometimes, by the choices you make, you can avoid falling into certain traps. But I'm talking about the kind of storms that hit you just because it's *life*.

Like the weather, there are certain circumstances we don't have a lot of control over. If you're dealing with such a storm right now, then I pray that this chapter really blesses your life.

Bottom line: Because there's a lot of stuff that happens that you can't necessarily avoid, there are challenges you're simply going to have to deal with.

PREPARATION IS THE KEY

Since things are going to happen, the best thing we can do is cultivate a mindset and attitude that will lend to a *positive* perspective. Many of the most successful gurus tell us that it's not about what happens *to* you, it's what happens *in* you. In other words, what matters is what you *do* about it.

For example:

Two people get laid off from the same company.

One decides to go home and shoot himself because he doesn't know how he's going to provide for his family, retire at a reasonable age, and do all the things he wants to do. He concludes: "I lost my job and my life is over." Boom.	The other goes home and decides to start his own business doing the same thing he just got fired from. He grows his business over two decades to the point where it's so successful, he buys the company that laid him off 20 years ago.

What's the difference between the two people? Clearly, it's not what happened *to* them, but rather what happened *in* them. One decided that because he went through a storm, his life was over. The other saw the storm as an opportunity for something better on the other side. It's your attitude, your mindset, your perspective toward what you're dealing with that matters the most. To that end, I want to equip you with a few strategies you can utilize to be prepared for life's challenges.

Delatorro L. McNeal, II

1. **Educate yourself by observation.**

   Whether you're in the middle of a storm or not, one of the best things you can do is learn from others. When you hear about someone—whether through conversation with friends, watching the news, or reading a magazine, newspaper, or book—who's been through a challenging time or adversity, I want you to ask a more profound question than *What happened?* I want you to ask *why* it happened, and then focus on how they got out of it or rebounded from the setback.

   When you begin to educate yourself on handling challenges, one of the things you'll learn is that many of the most successful people—in every career and life situation you can envision—have had to deal with storms at one time or another.

   List 3 people/situations you've read or heard about where the person handled a challenge in a positive way.

   _____

   _____

   _____

   _____

   _____

   _____

   _____

   _____

   _____

   _____

   _____

   _____

2. **Read and listen consistently to something positive that reinforces who you are.**

It's vital to be confident in how strong you are, how much your life means, and how valuable you are. If the storm comes and you're not solid in yourself, you'll be scurrying to brave the challenge. And my friend, I don't want you to scurry. The reason I want you to consistently be reading and listening to something positive that reinforces who you are is because every time you face a storm financially, emotionally, physically, health-wise, relationship-wise, or otherwise, it eats away at your confidence. If you're not prepared, challenges can diminish your belief in yourself and shatter your goals and dreams.

Knowing that the possibility of adversity exists, focus on making positive deposits into the bank account of your heart, mind, and spirit so that when challenges come (because they may come one at a time or in teams), you have enough in your account so that the storm doesn't bankrupt you.

List 3–5 books, articles, or movies you've read or watched that have had a positive impact on you and/or have helped you to build confidence in yourself.

_____

_____

_____

_____

_____

My book recommendations for you:

Failing Forward by John Maxwell

Turn Setbacks into Greenbacks by Willie Jolley

Unstoppable by Cynthia Kersey

Thriving Through Your Storms by Delatorro McNeal, II   ✔

Delatorro L. McNeal, II

3. **Keep champions in your life at all times.**

    Notice I didn't say keep successful or wealthy people, or those who
    have big houses and fat rides, or the most gorgeous or connected
    person you know in your life at all times. I said *champions*. Why?

    > Champions are positive, solid, quality, driven, passionate
    > people of excellence who have been through tough times
    > too and who believe in your success.

    They're important because:

    ✦ They keep you focused.

    ✦ They consistently think good thoughts toward you and pray
       for you.

    ✦ They continually encourage you.

    ✦ They rally around you.

    And here's another thing I love that champions do: They don't let
    you get too high when things are great or go too low when things are
    bad. In short, they keep you levelheaded.

    ✎ List 5–8 people you know who you would consider to be your
    champions. Put a star by those who are already in your life; note the
    others as those you might ask to become a champion for you.

    _____

    _____

    _____

    _____

    _____

Dr. Lee Jones was one of my mentors in college, and I took the power of his statement and realized that a champion doesn't get on their high horse, becoming arrogant and cocky about who they are and all they've accomplished. No "Ooow, lah-tee-dah, I'm just the bomb, it's all about me.com." They're an anchor in your life who keeps you in

> "Things are never really as good or as bad as they appear. They're often somewhere in the middle."
>
> —Dr. Lee Jones

check. And when things get rough, they refuse to let you slip down. They're the ones who pull you up and say: "You know what, things aren't that bad."

4. **Create an Emergency Fund.**

   Dave Ramsey in his bestselling book *Extreme Money Makeover* talks about the importance of having $1,000 liquid cash in an account as a basic emergency fund to handle unexpected storms in life that come to attack your finances.

   Let's be real for a moment: Almost 100% of the time, money may not solve your storm, but it does tend to do one of two things:

   ✦ It gives you more options and avenues to deal with your storms.

   ✦ It makes living through your storms more bearable and/or comfortable.

   So while things are going great in your life, don't live like difficult times will never come. Plan for good days and for rainy days. With this small emergency fund, you can handle some situations without going into credit card debt or having to pull from your investments.

5. **Help someone else through their difficult time.**

   If things are going great in your life, pay it forward by helping someone you know who's going through a tough time. Help them find a job, rebuild their credit, find better schools for their kids, start their business, or expand their circle of influence. Be there to listen, advise, encourage, and support them, and do it with sincerity and humility because you never know when you'll need someone to be there for you.

6. **Volunteer.**
One of the best things you can do to gain perspective on your storms is to serve those who have it much worse than you do. It will help you put your issues in proper perspective, and it will immediately shift your cognitive energy from that of complaining to an attitude of gratitude.

Let's say you're going through a money storm and you had to downgrade to a small apartment for a short season of your life. Instead of complaining about it, take one weekend and volunteer at a homeless shelter. You will quickly realize just how good you really have it.

> "People who have come before you and have had less than you have done better than you."
> —Maya Angelou

Because life's going to give you some highs and it's going to give you some lows, you need to try to stay somewhere in the middle if possible. Here are a couple of things to think about to help bring that idea home:

◆ When you know it's storming outside, you put on different shoes. Why? So that you have the necessary traction. Likewise, you wear the proper clothing to protect you (you wouldn't wear a suede jacket when you know you could ruin it and it's going to take forever to dry, right?). Or you wear light, breathable clothing that dries quickly. Because guess what? When it rains it pours. But you know what else? Your clothes eventually dry.

So why is it important for you to put the right shoes and outfit on? So that you're not overwhelmed by the challenges—you have some degree of preparation in place that shifts the focus away from the negative.

✦ Now think about this: When you're out in the rain, even with the umbrella and the right clothes, you still get wet. But what's the first thing you do when you get home? You take all the wet stuff off, hang it up to dry, and put on some nice, dry clothing.

Here's the interesting thing: After it's rained on you, and you're now cozy, maybe watching a movie and having something good to eat, you feel better. Why? Because that rain took you through a process that you were prepared for as best as possible, and now you can enjoy what comes afterward.

My friend, if you're going to thrive through your storms, you've got to have a game plan and a blueprint, because it's not so much what you're going *through*, it's what you're going *to* that counts.

Keep champions in your life. They make all the difference in the world. The only thing worse than going through a storm is going through one by yourself. You can survive any storm if you've got enough good quality people around you, because guess what? While it's raining outside, you can have a party inside. You can throw on some music, light some candles, cook some food, and have some friends come over to celebrate life while it's storming outside.

Remember what you cannot avoid, you must be prepared for. Think: *I couldn't avoid this particular storm, so I'm going to let it do what it does, because reality is, it's not going to rain all the time. The sun is coming out again.*

The sun is coming out in your situation as well.

CHAPTER SUMMARY

Since challenges will inevitably come your way, the best strategy is to prepare yourself by:

- ✦ Identifying people who've dealt with challenges in a way that inspires you.

- ✦ Utilizing books, magazines, audios, and movies that reinforce your self-worth and value in the world.

- ✦ Determining those around you who are now—or could become—champions in your life.

- ✦ Building up a $1,000 emergency fund.

- ✦ Reaching out to someone struggling and helping in any way you can.

- ✦ Serving others worse off than you through volunteering.

Massive Action Plan

Write down your action plan for preparing for a storm in your life based on what you learned from this chapter.

Failure 101

THRIVING THROUGH YOUR STORMS

2

FAILURE IS AN EVENT,
NOT A PERSON

Here is the course you never took in school but have been learning all your life. In fact, I firmly believe that much of our educational system doesn't teach many of the most important things we need to know in order to live a successful, fulfilling life, and one of those things is *failure*.

As I travel across the country, speaking to corporations, professional associations, colleges, conventions, churches, civic groups, and non-profit organizations, my goal is always this: to educate. Through my books, keynotes, seminars, training programs, interviews, websites, and social media, everything about me is focused on education.

As someone who attended great schools and attained both college and graduate degrees, I've self-taught, self-studied, learned, and read hundreds of books; I've also been through various courses and training programs. But nowhere did they teach me about adversity and overcoming obstacles. No one offered a class on failure. Despite that absent course offering, however, all throughout my life, I've been learning the material, as have you.

> "Failure is not an option; it is a privilege reserved exclusively for those who try."
> —Albert Einstein

I'm sure that somewhere along the way you've read or heard that "failure is not an option." Perhaps it came from an athletic coach before the big meet or game, or from your parents before you went to school as they encouraged you to be studious and involved in class. "Failure is not an option" is a pretty common phrase; but Einstein took it a step further by saying, "it's a privilege reserved." Why is it not an option to experience failure? Because it's an honor reserved exclusively for those who try.

I love something that Robert Kiyasaki said: "The reason why I'm more successful than most is because I failed more than most." Think about that for a moment. See, if you're not failing, if you're not experiencing any difficulties or disappointments, if you're not going through any storms, trials, or setbacks in life, you're not trying hard enough. Because as you try, you're likely going to experience adversity, whether on the way to something big or to something small. So at the end of the day, you need to make a decision:

> If I'm going to experience some level of hardship on the way—no matter the size of the goal—I might as well go for the big.

You can't fail if you don't try; and my friend, I want to commend, applaud, celebrate, and high-five you right now for trying. Many times we don't hear that someone's proud of us for attempts we make, but as your coach, consultant, friend, and mentor, I want you to know that I am. Whether you tried your best on a job, a new business opportunity, a friend-

CHAPTER 2 | FAILURE 101

ship, your grades, or getting over a painful situation from your past, at least you gave it a shot, even if the outcome wasn't what you hoped.

Have you ever noticed how we applaud babies who try and fail, but we tend not to applaud adults who try and fail? When was the last time you saw a baby learning how to walk? He or she wobbled from knees to feet, staggering while taking that first step, then took that second step and fell down. Did you say: "Aww, you failed, you fell down. Stay face in floor, go ahead and just stay down." No, you said: "Get back up again and keep trying." Because you know the more a child tries and fails, soon they're going to try and succeed, exponentially and perpetually.

Failure is not an option; it is a privilege reserved exclusively for those who try. I personally want to applaud you for trying, because so many people aren't even in the game, but my friend, you *are.* And to that end, I'm going to teach you seven principles that will change the way you think about failure from here on out.

PRINCIPLE #1

You will fail your way to success.

I've written five books to date, but if you were to ask my mom—or anybody in my family—if I would have been a bestselling author, they would have said no, because I didn't have strong writing skills as a child. Likewise, I'm a speaker and peak performance expert, but the first speech I gave sounds nothing close to the way I deliver on platforms across the nation today. In both arenas, I failed my way to success.

✎ Think about all the things you're successful at. List your top three.

_____

_____

_____

Now ask yourself: Was I really good at these when I first started out? Probably not.

Delatorro L. McNeal, II

> The late, great Luther Vandross—may he rest in peace—was booed off of Showtime at the Apollo three times and told he would never ever make it in the music business.

I can give you litanies of people throughout history who experienced failure on the road to success, so instead of looking at challenge and change as your foe, look at them as friends because they teach you things you never would have learned had you not encountered them.

PRINCIPLE #2

Failure is an event not a person.

Please, never again let me or anyone else catch you calling yourself a failure. When was the last time you went up to somebody, shook their hand, and introduced yourself as a failure? I imagine the answer is "never" because that's not who you are. You're *you*, not *failure*.

I don't care if you've failed at grades, money, relationships, business, love, romance, friendships, ministry, career, goals, or even in your dreams, hopes, and purpose. Don't let your calamity become your identity, and don't identify yourself by what you haven't been successful at. Failure is not a person or who you are. It's merely an event, so go ahead and leave it there as such. I guarantee that whatever it is, you can move beyond it, soar, and climb over it.

PRINCIPLE #3

Failure is a detour, not a dead end.

My friend, I don't care what you experience or go through in your life, there's always a way around it. Here's what I mean: Have you ever followed the GPS system in your car and then abruptly decided you were smarter, veering off to go your own way? And what does the system say when you do that? It doesn't shout: "Hey you stupid idiot, I can't believe you did that!" No. It says: "Off route … Recalculating," and reroutes you to get you back on course.

I want you to understand something: No matter where you've gotten off track, for whatever reason, that failure is the *detour*. Ok, you got off route; ok, it's going to take you a little bit longer to get where you're trying to go. Instead of your arriving in thirty minutes, you might get there in forty-five; rather than two years, it might take you three. It's a detour, not a dead end; it's a comma, not a period.

✎ List three detours you've recently encountered in your life that have changed your path to a goal.

_____

_____

_____

_____

_____

_____

PRINCIPLE #4

All failure you learn from becomes a life lesson.

The moment you embrace the reality of: *Hey, I might have gone through something, but guess what? I learned something from it*, your pain and tough times look a lot different. With this mindset, you're able to:

✦ Be more clear about what you want.

✦ Have a better strategy for how you go after the things you want.

Take relationships for example. If you continue to date the same type of person who isn't good for you, you haven't learned that in order to change the mate, you've got to change the bait. It's therefore vital to identify what those qualities are that keep attracting them to you—and you to them—and then learn how to spot them instantly so you can avoid them. In short, you have to make wiser choices.

So phrase your setbacks as comebacks by framing them as life lessons. Whether it's a job you lost, problems with the IRS, or perhaps estrangement within your own family, learn to implement tactics that will keep you from repeating that negative experience. Perhaps you need to re-evaluate your work ethic, your financial habits, or shed hurt or embarrassment from the past and find a way to reconnect.

Remember principle #2: Failure is an event not a person; and #3: Failure is a detour, not a dead end. My friend, I want you to adopt a mindset that says you're going to learn from everything. All failure that you learn from becomes a life lesson.

PRINCIPLE #5

Failure is fertilizer.

I learned from Dr. Denis Waitley that *fertilizer stinks, but it grows green people.* I think that's so powerful and true because the reality is, my friends, that failure comes to us to accelerate our lives. When people who've been through adversity, challenges, and change handle them right, they ascend to a whole other level of success much faster than those who've never been through failure and hardship. Why?

Because when you become wiser, you begin to see more that you can tap into. You're then able to take more risks to get where you want and need to be.

So failure is a fertilizer (and we know what that stuff is made of), and it does stink, just like failure. No one's claiming it doesn't stink:

- ✦ To go through hardship and painful times

- ✦ To lose friends, money, a career position, property, or 401K or retirement funds

- ✦ When the market is down, the economy is bad, and gas prices are through the roof

- ✦ When you can barely pay your bills, have insufficient funds notices, or must file bankruptcy

- ✦ When you go through divorce

- ✦ When you're diagnosed with a condition or disease

- ✦ When people lie to you, betray you, or cheat on you

- ✦ When you've been looked over time and again for that promotion

- ✦ When you're stuck in a position and can't quit

We've all experienced some or all of these things, and while they're definitely fertilizer in our lives, they grow green people.

Think about it: When fertilizer hits the soil, what happens? It catapults the growth, nutrients, strength, and vitality of the roots of whatever you're growing, making it greener, stronger, healthier, and more vibrant. It grows like wildfire. With a lawn especially, you can spot one that's fertilized vs. one that isn't, because the fertilizer keeps that lawn looking amazing even when bad weather comes.

I guarantee you that every person you know who's successful is a green person. If you ask them to open up the trunk of their trials, they will show you a lot of fertilizer. When we say, "Man, that grass looks green over there," we say that because we tend to think the grass is greener on the other side, right? But we don't understand that there's more fertilizer over there too. So before you say: "Oh, I want that person's life," or "Oh, I want to be like them," remember everything that shines isn't silver and everything that glitters isn't gold.

Delatorro L. McNeal, II

✎ List 3–5 challenges you've experienced in your life that you consider your fertilizer.

_____

_____

_____

_____

_____

PRINCIPLE #6

When you fail, learn from it, teach from it, and keep moving forward.

Whatever your storm is, strive to learn from it. Then after you decipher the lesson, share it with someone else and quickly move in a forward direction.

I take my daughters Miracle and Hope to playgrounds a lot, and one of the things I've taught them is that as soon as they experience a failure or disappointment on the playground, they do again exactly what they just failed at. Imagine Miracle is coming across the monkey bars and she lets go of her grip too soon, causing her to hit her head on one of the beams on the way down. Ouch! That hurts. So I hold her and wipe her tears, but then guess what? I don't let her leave until she does that same activity again successfully. I give her strategies on how to succeed, and when she finally does, I give her all the praise and applause I possibly can. Why do I do this? Because I never want her to leave a point of failure and look at it as such. I want her to learn from it, teach from it, and keep moving forward. My friend, you've got to do the same thing.

Here are a few examples you can use for motivation:

You experienced a financial failure. That doesn't mean you're never going to be able to get a credit card again. *Recoup and rebuild your credit and apply for another credit card later on.*

You had a setback in a class. That doesn't mean you're not college or graduate school material. *Take another course.*

That relationship didn't work out. It doesn't mean you'll never find "the one." *Heal yourself and let a new relationship come into your life.*

Your new business didn't work. A large percentage of small businesses are unsuccessful. *Learn what didn't work, become smarter, and give it another try.*

PRINCIPLE #7

Ultimately, there is no real failure; there's only feedback.

I'm going to close with this one because I want you to understand something: Although we've used the word *failure* throughout this chapter, in truth, failure doesn't actually exist. What does exist is *feedback*.

Let's use this example to illustrate: Let's say you get a medical diagnosis that isn't what you wanted or expected. It doesn't mean you're a failure or that you can't continue to have a great life. It means your body is giving you feedback that something isn't operating properly. You can now utilize this feedback to make better choices about your body.

Same thing goes for relationships. Don't look at your significant other or your spouse giving you some challenging words as, "Oh my gosh, it's over. I can't deal with this anymore." No. It's feedback, and with it you can make changes and better choices that make the relationship stronger.

If you look at every failure as feedback for where you need to make adjustments to help you succeed the next time, you'll find yourself ahead of the game.

I recorded a coaching video many years ago called "Take the Shot," where I use basketball as a metaphor.

make the shot ⤳ miss ⤳ adjust ⤳

shoot again ⤳ miss ⤳ adjust again ⤳ make it!

Every time you miss, do you just stop and go home? No, you grab the ball and try again because you understand that it's not failure, it's feedback.

✎ Consider the following categories and write down how you might be failing in some or all of them. Then jot down how you can use the feedback to make an improvement. For example:

Bank Account — *consistently low*
Need to change how I'm making money or managing my budget.

Friends —

_____

_____

Co-workers —

_____

_____

Boss —

_____

_____

Business —

_____

_____

Bank Account —

_____

_____

Course in School —

_____

_____

Relationship —

_____

_____

Other —

_____

_____

Keep in mind that if you reject the feedback you're receiving in any one area of your life, you're destined to repeat the same course and experience that exact failure again. The key to turning failure into feedback is to recognize the feedback, learn from it, then move forward powerfully with that new information so you can continue to become wiser. If you can learn to do that, you'll pass Failure 101 with flying colors!

CHAPTER SUMMARY

You now understand that *failure* doesn't actually exist; what you're accustomed to calling failure is really *feedback*. Learn to recognize this by:

- ✦ Identifying things you're successful at now and how you arrived at that level of achievement

- ✦ Determining the detours that changed your course and allowed you to land at a different destination

- ✦ Becoming clear on where the fertilizer has been sprinkled in your life and how it's growing your situation

- ✦ Realizing that those you think you envy may not be so enviable after all

- ✦ Recognizing areas where you failed the first time but ultimately achieved success

- ✦ Highlighting the areas of your life where feedback can help put you on a wiser path

Massive Action Plan

Write down your action plan based on what you learned from this chapter.

_____

_____

_____

_____

_____

_____

In the Storm

THRIVING THROUGH YOUR STORMS

3

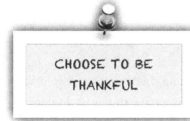

CHOOSE TO BE
THANKFUL

On a beautiful Tuesday afternoon, I was set to attend a mastermind meeting with a few of my fellow speaker entrepreneur friends. I live in Tampa, and this meeting was being held in Lakeland, which is about forty-five miles away and just under an hour's drive. Since the weather was great, I decided to take my motorcycle (I love riding my motorcycle).

The meeting was a huge success—I learned a lot and was excited—but as I left, I looked out toward Tampa and saw a lot of storm clouds. My good buddy, Eric, looked at me and said: "Del, you're on your motorcycle, man, what are you going to do?"

"I'm going to drive home."

"Well, what happens when it rains?" he asked.

"I'm going to keep driving," I said. "I'll make it out. I'll be just fine."

"Ok, cool," he said. "Well, man, have a good one. Don't get too wet."

With a great attitude I got on my bike, put on my gear, and realized as I reached the I-4 intersection that I was low on gas. Then I heard the crackling of thunder and lightning. I was not one mile down the road when the sky unleashed a torrential downpour.

My friend, I was in a storm and had very little gas, so the first thing I knew I needed to do was get some fuel.

> In order to thrive through my storm,
> I had to drive through my storm.

So I exited and went to the first gas station, where a couple of people filling up their cars saw me. One said, "Man, you're drenched! Are you going to just stay here and wait it out?"

"Absolutely not," I said. "I've got somewhere to go and I'm going to get there." I took off my soaked helmet and gloves and filled my tank. After I finished and put my wet gear back on, somebody said: "Man, why don't you just stay here and wait it out?"

"Because," I said, "I have no clue how long this storm's going to last. And I have more profitable, powerful, and productive things to do than sit in the middle of the storm."

With that, I mounted my bike, cranked up the ignition, and made a decision that I was going to drive straight from Lakeland back to Tampa. No matter how bad it was raining, I was going to do it. Why? Because I wanted to thrive though my storm.

So while I was at the red light waiting to get back on I-4, I said to myself: *What are some things I can do to transform this challenging experience into something that would be kind of cool...to turn this setback into a comeback, this adversity into an opportunity...to turn forty-five minutes worth of what most people would consider hell riding on a motorcycle in a torrential downpour into something positive?*

With my helmet fogging up every ten seconds—I had to keep the lid down or the rain would hit me dead in the face—it wasn't easy. But I thought: *I'm in a storm but I've got fuel.*

My friend, if you're going to make it through your storms, you've got to have fuel in order to stay encouraged, inspired, uplifted. There's no way I would have made it if I didn't stop and get gas. So what does that mean for you? Think about the fuel that nurtures your soul:

✦ What books do you need to be reading?

✦ What relationships do you need to hold onto?

✦ What Scriptures or quotes do you need to be memorizing?

✦ What tapes, books, and/or sermons do you need to constantly pour into your mind to keep yourself uplifted?

✎ Can you think of any situations in which you were in a storm yet had "fuel"? What kept you going? What was/is your fuel?

_____

_____

_____

_____

_____

When I made up my mind to transform my experience, I decided that for every car that passed me, I was going to give them a thumbs up, smile at them, and wave to lift their spirits from driving in a storm. I also decided that I was going to sing some of my favorite songs. Now, on a sunny day I can turn on my iPod and pop in the earbuds to listen to great music; but when I was in the storm, I couldn't do that, so I chose to sing. I picked out four or five of my favorite songs and became my own DJ.

Delatorro L. McNeal, II

What did I do in my situation? I used what's called the **flip-switch technique**. Here's what that means:

> In the middle of whatever you're going through, you have to instantaneously choose your attitude and state of mind.

If you're in a place you don't want to be mentally, emotionally, physically, or spiritually, you have the power to change it in an instant. You see, just like when you come into a dark room, you can flip a switch and that room immediately goes from dark to light. Well, guess what? Your thoughts work just as quickly. You can likewise immediately change how you're feeling by changing what you're focusing on. When I was in that storm, I knew the ride could either be hell or it could be heaven—it was all based on my mindset. If I wanted to, I could have focused on the multiple discomforts I was experiencing at the time:

+ I was cold.
+ I was soaking wet.
+ I was getting dirty from the mud kicking up, not only from my tires, but from everyone else's (and I was wearing a cool outfit!).
+ The rain was pelting my arms like bee stings (I didn't have my jacket with me because it was a 100 degree day in Florida).
+ Each minute felt like five minutes.
+ I could barely see in front of me.
+ I couldn't go top speed which meant it was going to take even longer to get home.

But, my friend, I didn't do that.

Have you ever been in a situation where you wanted to get somewhere —perhaps that next level in your life—but you had to slow down because of the storm? My friend, I've been there. My bike was built to go sixty or seventy miles an hour, but I couldn't do it that day. I could have dwelled on the fact that being caught in that storm was going to delay some of the other things I had planned, which meant I would be less productive that day. I could have focused on the drivers passing me who were comfortable and dry, playing their music. Some had company; I was by myself. But I didn't focus on any of those things—I used the flip-switch technique to put my attention on where I was going, not what I was *going through*.

Have you ever used the flip-switch technique to shift your attention away from something negative you were going through? If so, briefly jot the situation(s) down. What did you think about to change your focus? If not, imagine a situation where you could have used the technique and share what you would have done.

_____

_____

_____

_____

_____

As I set out on that ride, I made up my mind to be grateful for the wonderful opportunity to experience one of the phenomenons of nature. I was thankful that I had gasoline, that I could see as far as I could. I was grateful that I was on a reliable motorcycle that wouldn't break down on me. I was thankful for the fact that I had just met with some amazing friends who love me and want to help me grow my business. I appreciated having a nice home to go to and that I had songs in my heart and spirit I could sing. I felt gratitude for having a helmet because I was passing other motorcyclists who didn't, and I was thankful for having clothes on my body—they may have been wet, but I still had them. I was even thinking I was happy that I was wearing clean underwear, because my mama taught me when I was a little bitty boy: "Baby, make sure when you go out, you got on clean underwear. You never know if you're going to get into an accident and have to go to the hospital."

Knowing that in an instant I could shift my focus from negative to positive made all the difference. Did the rain stinging my arms hurt? Yes. But after about twenty minutes, my arms numbed up and I couldn't feel it anymore. I envisioned getting into a nice hot bubble bath and making myself a nice dinner, then snuggling up and watching an action-packed Netflix movie later on. I imagined getting some emails from people who had ordered one of my books, CDs, or programs; I even pictured somebody somewhere in the world reading one of my books and their life being transformed. I focused on the fact that every single time I saw a new green sign, the numbers for the miles were getting lower and lower— You're 50 miles from home … 40 … 30 … 20 … 10, 5, 4, 3, 2, 1.

✎ List 10 things you're grateful for at this moment in your life.

_____

_____

_____

_____

_____

_____

_____

_____

_____

_____

The amazing thing is simply this, my friend: When I changed what I focused on, and I got myself busy encouraging others by waving, giving thumbs up, smiling, and singing, I was home faster than I realized.

> Focus on your future,
> instead of on the pity party of your present.

Even more incredible than the speed with which I traveled, when I arrived home in Tampa, there wasn't a rain cloud in sight, only blue skies and sun. I pulled my motorcycle into the garage and said: "Thank you Lord that you kept me safe on the highways and the byways. Thank you for keeping my circle of friends on the highway and byway safe. Everybody who was on the road with me, thank you for keeping them safe; I pray they get to their destinations safely."

I took off my soaking wet helmet and gloves, dashed upstairs, tossed my wet clothes into the laundry, and took a nice, hot shower. You know, sometimes we take for granted the things we enjoy on a daily basis. That shower, dry clothes, air conditioning, a warm bed … they never felt so good.

My friend, I want to encourage you to use the flip-switch technique. In order to thrive through your storm, you have to:

+ Choose your attitude
+ Choose to be thankful
+ Choose to be positive
+ Choose your perspective

And in spite of the things that are going wrong around you, you have to choose to focus on what's going right in your life. Don't fall into the trap of saying: "Everything is going to hell in a hand basket." Don't use global terms like that. *Everybody. All.* I have *nothing* left. I've lost *everything.* Those all-encompassing terms aren't true. You haven't lost everything. Everybody doesn't hate you. You've got more going for you than you realize.

Extraordinary people go through extraordinary challenges. You're going to make it out of yours, but you've got to use the flip-switch

Delatorro L. McNeal, II

technique so that when you're feeling down, upset, disappointed, or rejected, you can choose in that moment to change to something positive. You might not be able to control what's happening *to* you, but you can control what's happening *in* you, and you can use what's happening *in* you to change the landscape.

> Remember, just because something is happening in the world, doesn't mean it has to happen in your world.

You see, even though it was raining in the world that day, it wasn't raining in *my* world. The sun was shining in my mind, heart, and spirit, and that was the weather I chose to focus on. Because I did the flip-switch and changed the weather that was happening *in* me, it helped me get through the weather that was happening all *around* me.

My friend, whatever it is that you're dealing with, know that it cannot rain all the time; the sun is coming out again. And the rising of the sun brings a lifting of your burdens day in and day out.

> When you change the way you look at things ...
> the things you look at change.
>
> —Dr. Wayne Dyer

CHAPTER SUMMARY

Utilizing the flip-switch technique will literally transform your life. It may take time before it becomes a habit, but focusing on the following will get you there:

- ✦ What are your "fuel" sources?

- ✦ How can you build up and/or add to those sources for ready use?

- ✦ What are you grateful for right now in your life?

- ✦ Think of times you've used the flip-switch to shift the negative to a positive.

- ✦ Don't use global terms like *everyone*, *nobody*, *all*, or *nothing* to describe your challenging situations.

- ✦ Remember that you might not be able to control what's happening *to* you, but you can control what's happening *in* you.

Massive Action Plan

Write down your action plan based on what you learned from this chapter.

_____

_____

_____

_____

_____

_____

Win/
Learn

THRIVING THROUGH YOUR STORMS

4

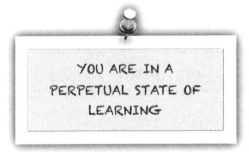

YOU ARE IN A
PERPETUAL STATE OF
LEARNING

Are you ready to experience a paradigm shift? I hope so, because I'm about to share something with you that you've likely never heard. After I read about this mindset, it changed my life and those of audiences all across the country and around the world, and it's going to change yours too.

Here it is: All successes are 80% psychology, 20% mechanics. And I'm here to teach you the 80 and the 20, not only how you can *think* so you can make it through your storms, but also how to *act*. It's the psychology that I call the reverse of win/lose.

All your life, you've been taught that either you win or you lose, right? Your parents, teachers, professors, and leaders have probably said: "Hey, go after whatever you want, but the reality is you're going to either win or you're going to lose."

Now here's the problem with this psychology: Its focus is strictly positive/negative.

> "You don't either win or lose."
>
> —George Fraser, author of Click: Ten Truths for Building Extraordinary Relationships

I've adopted the principle of my friend and mentor, George Fraser, and taken it a step further. Here is where I want you to get in the zone with me and think about a few things.

Have you ever won something, such as:

+ A race
+ A sporting event
+ A playstation or Wii game
+ A bet
+ A job opportunity
+ A board game
+ A trophy
+ An award

I'm pretty sure the answer is yes. Ok, so you've won before.

Have you ever lost something, such as:

+ Time
+ Money
+ Energy
+ Friends
+ Relationships
+ Opportunities
+ Funds
+ Career opportunities
+ Your mind
+ Your sense of belief and self-confidence
+ Your pride
+ Your sense of passion for life
+ Your direction

I'm sure you have.

Delatorro L. McNeal, II

See, the problem with win/lose psychology is that if I say anything you do in life is going to produce a positive or a negative result, your brain is immediately going to try to talk you out of anything that could produce a negative result for you. Why? Because your brain is very smart; it wants you to succeed. So it's going to sway you away from anything in which you haven't had prior success.

Let me ask you a question: Have you ever had an idea for something, and shortly after you got that creative intuition, your brain started coming up with the reasons why you couldn't pull it off? And as a result, you began to talk yourself out of trying?

Now why did that happen? Because as soon as you come up with a thought of something you want to accomplish, your brain instantly references one place to determine whether you'll succeed, and that place is your past. It looks over everything you've ever done in your life—high, low, good, or bad—then assesses if there's a prior example of success in that area. If not, your brain responds by saying: "Hey, hold on. Maybe you shouldn't go after that, because guess what? If you do, and you don't have previous success in it, chances are you probably aren't going to succeed in it."

> ## When things go wrong, don't go with them.
> —Les Brown

For this reason, it can be dangerous to dream entirely in your head because your brain is set up to help you succeed, so it will naturally want you to avoid "losing." Our mind sees losing as a negative, but I'm going to teach you a method of reprogramming your mind.

You've admitted to me that you've won in life and that you've lost. Now the reason why I say this chapter is going to be a paradigm shift for you is because I don't believe you should adopt a win/lose psychology. The truth is, we've all won and lost in life. But let me ask you a powerful question:

For everything in life you've ever lost,
did you at some point LEARN from it?

If the answer is yes—and if you think hard, you'll realize it always is—then we've got a new paradigm, because we don't either win or *lose*, we either win or *learn*. Now if I were in front of a live audience, I would do the *Matrix* moment right now and the whole audience would do it with me and say: "I-I-I-I got it!"

List 5 situations in your life where you've experienced a loss but have learned from it.

So wherever you are right now, I want you to say this to yourself:

> "In life, I don't either win or lose, I actually win or learn."

Excellent! Because, my friend, if you can adopt a win/learn psychology, you have automatically shifted from a positive/negative (win/lose) to a double positive. A win/learn.

Let me prove it to you. Are you afraid of winning? Absolutely not; you love to win. That's why you compete, why you get involved in the things you do, because you want to win. We all do. Now let me ask you another question: Are you afraid of learning? Absolutely not. You can't be afraid of learning. Why? Because you spent your entire life learning. From the time you came out of the womb, you've been learning every hour of every day. From the time you wake up to the time you go to sleep you're learning. Even while you're sleeping you're learning. Why? Because in dreaming you learn from your unconscious mind.

None of us is afraid of learning or afraid of winning. So if that's our reality, then we now have no excuse not to achieve our goals and dreams, to go after that new opportunity. Why? Because either you're going to win or you're going to learn. So why not:

- ✦ Start the business of your dreams.
- ✦ Pursue your education.
- ✦ Explore a new venture.
- ✦ Give those new friendships a try.
- ✦ Go after everything that God has put on the inside of your heart.

Either you're going to win or you're going to learn, so be assured that even when the storm comes and it's raining down on your head, you're learning all kinds of things. And as you learn you become wiser and able to better live your dreams at the highest level.

> All successes are 80% psychology, 20% mechanics.

CHAPTER SUMMARY

Shifting from a win/lose to a win/learn mentality is a surefire way to give you a whole new perspective on life. Trying something new will no longer fill you with fear of failure, but rather eagerness to learn; experiencing a loss will become a lesson. To hone this technique, keep these tips in mind:

- ✦ You're not afraid of winning.

- ✦ You're not afraid of learning.

- ✦ For everything you've lost, you've learned from it.

- ✦ Since you're either going to win or learn, you might as well go for it!

Massive Action Plan

Write down your action plan based on what you learned from this chapter.

You're Stronger than You Know

THRIVING THROUGH YOUR STORMS

5

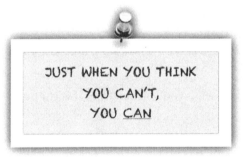

JUST WHEN YOU THINK
YOU CAN'T,
YOU CAN

I heard it said once that storms that come to make you strong make you weak first. I have to agree—adversity is the best personal trainer there is! That's why I say you have to realize you're human and give yourself permission to be down every now and again—the trick is not to get trapped there.

One of the things you can do to thrive through whatever storm you're experiencing is to *listen* to your struggle and your life, to what it's trying to show you and teach you. When you're able to do that, and when you employ the flip-switch technique I've taught you to put yourself in a better mental state, you'll find that each day you get a little bit stronger. Each time you persevere and make it in spite of the odds and obstacles pressing against you, you'll *feel* more empowered.

Storms that come to make you strong do make you weak first, and that's ok. But my friend, I don't want you to stop in your storm when the weakness sets in. You see, the drama in life we have to deal with is just like the weights we use when we work out. Exercise takes repetition and additional weight over time to build muscle and tone your body. Think about it: You don't build your chest by doing a bench press only one time; it normally requires three sets of 8–10 reps. As you push that weight away from you, you're building your muscles through repetition. And the more you work out, the more you learn: You learn that you're stronger than you know.

How many of you have ever been in a situation where you were working out with a friend, colleague, significant other, or trainer, and you got to number eight and they said: "Give me two more." And their motivation and excitement for you enabled you to do two more than you thought you could. Perhaps you've experienced this in other arenas too:

✦ You didn't think you could do any more, and your coach was able to get another lap out of you.

✦ You didn't think you could apply yourself any more, and your boss was able to get a better performance out of you.

✦ You didn't think you could give any more, and your pastor or spiritual leader was able to get some more servanthood out of you.

✦ You didn't think you could love any more, and then you had another child and realized how much more there was in you.

My friend, you're stronger than you know. But it takes being put in tough situations for us to understand how strong we really are. See, when life is going just dandy and there aren't any issues, you don't always need to draw on your strength. Why? Because you're coasting … things are fine; you're just chillin'. It's when you have difficult times that the strength comes in handy. It's why every successful person I've ever met has always said the same thing:

"I've learned more through failure than I have through success."

Delatorro L. McNeal, II

Let's face it: The tough times make us dig deep. Think about this proverb:

> "If you want to see what a tea bag is made out of,
> just put it in hot water."

It takes tough situations to steep the best out of us; we don't really see who we are as individuals until those circumstances arise. Scripture reminds us that God will never put more on us than we can handle; however, when it may feel like too much, I want you to make me a promise right now that you're not going to give up. You're going to fight back and push against those weights that are trying to get you to quit when:

+ You feel like giving up.
+ You're depressed.
+ You experience low self-esteem.
+ You imagine nobody's ever going to love you again.
+ You believe no one's ever going to give you an opportunity again.
+ You think you're never going to have good credit again.
+ You worry you're never going to make enough money again.
+ You're concerned you're never going to have a nice house again.
+ You assume your best days are behind you instead of ahead of you.
+ You're convinced that you're never going to _____.

Whatever it is that the enemy is trying to lie to you about, I want to encourage you to push it aside because your best is yet to come. As I've said before, extraordinary people go through numerous challenges, and whether you realize it or not, *you* are an extraordinary individual; your challenges are proof of that. So while other people, your job, your friends, or your current bank account balance might not be telling you that, I'm here to tell you that you are. So in order to thrive through your storm, my friend, you cannot stay stuck in the storm. You've got to drive through it.

"Ok, Del," you might say, "but what do you mean by that?" I'm so glad you asked.

See, we've all probably been on a road trip at one time or another. Being a Florida boy and having lived there all my life, I can attest to driving from one place to another and all of a sudden, it changes from blue sky to torrential downpour—so intensely that you can barely see twenty or thirty feet in front of you. And in those times, you often see people pull over to the shoulder or stop under an overpass. And I understand the reason they do that; they're saying: "I'm concerned about my driving ability, the visibility, the safety for myself and my family, so I'd rather just pull over to the side until it eases up. Then we can continue on and enjoy the rest of the journey without the worry of the storm."

I get that; it makes sense. However, the title of this book isn't *Sit and Let Your Storm Beat Up on You for the Rest of Your Life*. It's *Thriving Through Your Storms*. And if you're going to *thrive* through your storm, you've got to *drive* through your storm. So in the middle of your challenge, my friend, please don't shut down or call it quits. Put on your flashers to warn other people: *Hey, things aren't perfect, but I'm still moving*. You might not be going seventy miles an hour; instead you're going thirty. But because you're moving, you're going to get through much faster than if you just sat there.

List 3 challenges in your life that may have caused you to slow down but you didn't allow yourself to quit.

_____

_____

_____

_____

_____

_____

You were able to recall times you didn't quit, weren't you? It may have been difficult, but you did it. So the next time you doubt your ability to stay strong, I want you to use these examples to empower yourself.

The bottom line is: You've got a choice. You can thrive and drive or sit and wallow. Life is too short, so it's important for you to believe that where you're going *to* is worth what you're going *through*, that you've got enough in you to get you to blue skies again. So slow down, put on your hazard lights, windshield wipers, and some good, fun music. The more you stay engaged while you're going through a challenge, the faster and more powerfully you'll get through it. So stay active, stay busy, stay creative. Get your mind and heart off your issue and put it on your future.

Les Brown says it like this: "Get out of your head and into your greatness." I'm going to say it like this:

> "Get out of your problem and into your possibility."

My friend, you are stronger than you know. I'm going to ask you to give me a few more reps, a few more squats, a few more laps … because there's more in you than you realize. I need you to fight a little bit harder, to keep going and not stop in the storm. To *thrive* through your storm, you've got to *drive* through your storm.

CHAPTER SUMMARY

We've all experienced times where we felt hopeless and wondered how we would get through to a better phase of our lives. But if you look back and examine, you'll see that you *were* able to make it through when you thought it was impossible. It's vital to draw on that knowledge, on those times you've proven you're stronger than you thought possible. And when it's tough to do that (and I know sometimes it is), remember these tips from your buddy, Del:

- ✦ Slow down and breathe.

- ✦ Let people you trust help you through.

- ✦ Believe in the power of the difficult experience to strengthen you for the future.

- ✦ Have faith that you'll come through with more wisdom and empowerment (and maybe even a new opportunity) than you ever imagined possible.

Massive Action Plan

Write down your action plan based on what you learned from this chapter.

_____

_____

_____

_____

_____

_____

Delatorro L. McNeal, II

Thriving
Through
Loss

6

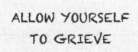

ALLOW YOURSELF
TO GRIEVE

Up until this year, I hadn't lost a member of my immediate family in over ten years, so I could sympathize but not truly empathize with those who had to thrive through the storm of death. But on April 30, 2013, my mother unexpectedly passed away.

At that point, I realized I couldn't write a book on overcoming obstacles and adversity without including a chapter on how to thrive during one of the hardest personal tragedies a person can deal with—the loss of the person who gave them life.

While the pain is immeasurable, I'm comforted in knowing that Olivia B. Fatherly—my mother of thirty-six years—is now resting in peace and enjoying the beauty and splendor of heaven. I will be forever grateful to her for giving me a chance at life and for sacrifices she made that I'll never know about. My mother loved my brother Michael and me so much that she abandoned many of her dreams so that we could live ours. She always said that her greatest achievement wasn't her education, her wealth, her ability to speak, her houses in the suburbs, or her leadership positions in the church; rather, she boasted about raising "Her Guys." My brother and I, of course, believed her greatest achievement was that of being an amazing mom. The truth is that my life would not be nearly what it is today if it weren't for her. I've been blessed to touch millions of lives, and I will continue to do so because of my mom.

If you're reading this chapter and you've experienced the loss of a loved one, I would personally like to say that I am truly sorry for your loss. I honestly know how you feel, and I pray that with time your heart will heal, that you'll find peace, rest, comfort, solace, and joy—emotionally and spiritually—in the fact that your loved one is in a better place.

I don't consider myself an expert on this subject by any means, but living through this process gives me the ability to at least share a few things that helped me and that I know have helped many others cope with the pain of loss.

1. When you're grieving, don't try to be strong; rather, be authentic with your feelings.

So often, people who aren't experiencing the loss that you are at the time try to convince you to be strong. In other words, they try to steer you away from what you're feeling in the moment. The problem with this is that it doesn't allow you to feel authentically. Emotions are good; they're meant to serve you. I can't tell you how many people I've talked to who admitted they never got a chance to really grieve for their loved one. Because everyone around them was convincing them to be strong, by the time they got a chance to be authentic with their emotions, their loved one's funeral service was long over and they felt it was too late.

Don't let well-meaning family and friends talk you out of the time you need to process what has just transpired in your life. The loss of someone close to you is just that—a loss. So be real with yourself and express how you feel. It's okay to say: "I'm hurting," "This is painful," "This isn't fair," "Why so soon?" and the like. It's okay to grieve. In order to thrive through your storm, you can't act as if you're not in one. Simply accept it and allow yourself to grieve.

2. Allow people who love you to comfort you, support you, and pray for you.

Because many people are probably asking how you are, it's important not to give the typical knee-jerk response of "I'm fine," because you're not. Sometimes we actually block our own blessings by not allowing people close to us to serve us during our time of need, so let people support you. Don't try to be a superhero. Allow people to cook for you, drive you places, help out around the house, accompany you to important meetings, and simply be there for you.

When people ask you if you need anything, don't be afraid to ask for prayers, both for you and your loved one. Most people want to help but are unsure what to do, so give them something to do on your behalf to help you make it through this difficult time. Welcome the love and the care—I find that most people are better at giving than receiving. When you're grieving the loss of a loved one, it's your time to receive.

3. Focus on your loved one's gain, rather than your loss.

It's natural that when someone dies, we tend to focus on *our* loss. We're acutely aware that we can no longer talk to them, laugh with them, take trips with them, snuggle with them, celebrate with them, or simply enjoy life with them as we did while they were alive. And although those things are true, it's also important to keep in perspective what that person gained by transitioning out of this life.

Anyone who knows me is aware that I'm a person of great faith and believe in heaven. When my mother passed it hurt like crazy, but every time I felt depressed and sad, I started thinking about her *gain* and it helped me. I started envisioning her in heaven with all of her family and friends who had gone before her, and the party she was now able to enjoy up there. In fact, just a few days after my mother's passing, I was inspired to write a poem that would appear on her funeral program. I imagined her sitting in heaven, and I wrote what I believed she would say to us here on earth now that she was there. By putting the focus on her gain rather than my loss, it truly shifted my viewpoint on her transition by allowing me to understand what a better place she was in now that she was with the Lord.

With this illustration in mind, I want you to think about how you can focus on all that your loved one has gained, rather than what you've lost by their absence. As you do so, may you be comforted by the verse that states: "To be absent from the body is to be present with the Lord." (2 Corinthians 5:8)

4. Send your loved one home first class.

One of the things I truly believe aids in the process of thriving through loss is how much effort you put into making your loved one's Homegoing celebration a wonderful experience. If the person meant a lot to you, send them home first class. Now, I don't mean break the bank, but make their celebration excellent by giving it your best effort.

When my mother passed, my brother and I set out to plan a celebration for her that was worthy of the life she led and the legacy she was leaving for us to follow. I personally made it my mission to plan her funeral service with the same detail, precision, and excellence as I would any of my live seminars, conferences, or events. I even set out to incorporate video and photo slideshows into the program because that's what she was used to seeing from me.

So when it came to planning her Homegoing, Michael and I went big —not expensive, but first class in terms of elements of the program we knew she would want. People talked about my mother's funeral for months

Delatorro L. McNeal, II

after it was over, and every time someone said, "Your mother would have been so proud of how her boys sent her home," it healed me and made me smile.

So my friend, if your loved one meant a lot to you, express it in the way you plan the celebration of their life, giving it the same level of excellence you would your job, your business, or anything else you love or adore.

5. Realize that you did the best you could.

This one is tough, but critically important. The number one thing that hits every person who grieves over the loss of a loved one is a feeling of regret about not doing more for that person while they lived. And let me tell you, sometimes it can take years for that feeling to go away; for some people, it never does.

Now, I'm not trying to convince you that you won't have this feeling or be plagued by these questions, but if you lived a life that honored the person you lost and tried diligently to take good care of that person while you were blessed to have them in your life, then at some point you have to be able to say the following and mean it:

"I did the best I could."

Now, say it again.

"I did the best I could."

Now, close your eyes, put your hands over your heart, and think of your loved one while saying it one more time.

"I did the best I could."

My friend, here's the truth: Not one of us wakes up each morning, turns the barometer of our life to average, and then goes to live it. I truly believe that most people get up every day and do the best they can with the knowledge and skills they have at the time. So although plenty of nagging thoughts will come no matter how much you gave to your loved one, give yourself grace. Be gentle with yourself; hindsight is always 20/20, and no amount of "shoulda, coulda, wouldas" will bring your loved one back, so take comfort in the quality of life you were able to provide for them, reminding yourself that you did the best you could.

6.   Know that each day you will get a little stronger, but you will still have "moments."

I agree that time heals all wounds, but when it comes to loss, everyone has "moments." As you learn to rebuild and continue your life without your loved one's physical presence, know in your heart that you'll get stronger as each day passes, but you'll also have moments. Any number of triggers can occur: a song, a location, a person, a situation, a smell, a commercial, a movie, a vacation spot, a website, a phone call, a photo, a room, a house, a car, a hospital, the weather, another family … just about anything will remind you of something significant about the person you've lost. At times, your heart will flutter and tears will flow, but that's completely natural, healthy, and normal.

I've had moments, while in the middle of a flight, when something triggers the thought of my mother and I quietly begin to cry. When it happens, I put my shades on, turn to the corner, and allow myself to miss her for a few moments; then I wipe the tears away and am fine. Other times, I can look at numerous photos of her in an album and not shed a single tear.

Emotion is unpredictable, so know you'll get stronger as the days go by, but give yourself some grace for the "moments."

7.   Know that your loved one is truly in a better place.

I don't know your specific situation or how you lost your loved one, but I lost my mother to health challenges. It therefore helps me heal when I realize she is no longer in pain. Although my mother never smoked, drank, did drugs, or even cursed, she fought major health challenges for the majority of my adult life. I often had to watch her live in and out of hospitals and doctors' offices, and she suffered from a lot of pain. But no matter how uncomfortable she was, when you asked her how she was doing, she always responded the same: "Oh Child ... I'm truly blessed!"

I know that we want our loved ones around as long as possible, but when they're living in pain on a daily basis, it's actually selfish of us to ask them to stay here on earth just to be there for us—especially when they have a pain-free heaven into which they can transition. It has helped me greatly to realize that my mother likely wouldn't come back even if she had the option and that "Earth has no sorrow that heaven can't heal."

My friend, your loved one is in a place of beauty and serenity now, so in the midst of the hurt, pain, and devastation you might feel, take comfort in knowing that if they had a relationship with God, they are truly living in a better place.

8.   Create something that honors their life.

Life is a powerful force. There is nothing that can replace the brilliance of the life of someone we loved and lost; however, we can give life to something in their absence that brings about change, hope, peace, and good will.

I want you to consider what you can do that will honor the legacy of the person you've lost. Ask yourself what you can create, start, build, design, launch, execute, organize, assemble and/or develop that can stand as a memorial to the person you love and miss so much. Perhaps one of the following will resonate with you as an idea:

✦ Write a book and dedicate the book to your loved one.

✦ Start a support group and name it after your loved one.

✦ Donate to a charity in the name of your loved one.

✦ Build a website that honors the life and legacy of your loved one.

+ Begin a non-profit organization and name it after your loved one.

+ Create a scholarship fund in honor of your loved one.

+ Plant trees and name the field or the land after your loved one.

+ Start a business in honor of your loved one.

+ Develop a local, regional, or even national program to help fight the disease/challenge that took the life of your loved one.

My friend, the possibilities are endless, but I hope you see the point here. If you can find some way to pull purpose from your pain, you can actually effect positive change in this world in honor of your loved one.

9. Realize that your greatest impression on them was the life you led.

This one is difficult. I've talked to many people who share with me the same frustration I still feel to some degree to this day, and it stems from the fact that their loved one passed away at a moment when they couldn't say goodbye.

Some people spend months—even years—taking care of their loved one, and when the final transition happens, not being there is simply heartbreaking. Others lose someone in an accident or unfortunate life event, and not being physically there when they take their last breath can be a pain that is difficult to process and heal from.

My brother and I cared for our mother every step of the way, yet on that Tuesday, the Lord chose to call her home during a window of time when neither my brother nor I could be at the nursing facility. By the time we both arrived at the emergency room, she was already gone. For the life of us, we couldn't figure out why she didn't hold out for us to be by her side when she transitioned to heaven, but we had to trust that God took her home for His purpose and in His time, not ours.

For a while, I was angry that I didn't get a chance to say my final goodbye to my mother, but what I have since come to understand is that the way I lived my life while she was here was the strongest impression I could make on her. I tried valiantly to be the best son, to make her proud of the man she had raised and for whom she had sacrificed so much. I strove to care tenderly for her every day I spent time with her—even bringing her home-cooked meals—and I did my best to honor her in my presentations by utilizing all she taught me. Ultimately, I've come to terms with not being there in her final moments of transition, believing that my life was my goodbye.

So my friend, I want you to know that if your loved one passed away during a time when you stepped away to get something to eat, or went home to get some sleep, or took a necessary trip, or simply weren't there when it happened, the life you led was the strongest and most lasting impression they had of you during their final moments. I believe they thought good thoughts toward you, that they loved and appreciated you for all you did for them, and that if they could come back and tell you that, they would.

Tears…

10. Be thankful that you had as much time with that person as you did.

Finally, it's important to realize that you are a blessed individual to have had your loved one in your life. Between the months of April and September 2013, my immediate family experienced the loss of three prominent family members: my mother, my godfather (Dr. Arthur T. Jones), and my great uncle (Charlie Ball, Sr.) who was like a grandfather to me. Processing three deaths in a six-month timeframe was extremely challenging for our family; however, the one theme that continued to resonate among us was an overwhelming sense of gratitude for the life and legacy of each of these amazing people.

Would we have relished our loved ones' being here on earth much longer than they were? Absolutely. But we realized we were blessed to have been born into a family that allowed us to be connected to them for as long as we were—some as long as sixty years.

So the point, my friend, is this: Count your blessings. Realize that although their life here on earth has concluded, they didn't transition without leaving you with a tremendous amount of wealth in terms of their wisdom, life lessons, memories, fun times, laughter, smiles, help, voice of support, prayers for you, advice when you needed it most, and many other things. But rather than talk about this concept of gratitude, let's experience it right here, right now.

On the line below, I want you to write the name of a loved one you've lost and are thinking about right now. Then, I want you to complete each sentence I've started for you. These will help you express sincere gratitude for the impact your loved one had on your life and to reflect on all the wealth they have now left in your care.

My loved one's name is:

_____

Right now, I am so grateful because he/she...

Taught me how to:

_____

_____

_____

_____

Showed me how to:

_____

_____

_____

_____

Delatorro L. McNeal, II

Provided me with:

_____

_____

_____

_____

Told me to always:

_____

_____

_____

_____

Reminded me that:

_____

_____

_____

_____

Protected me from:

_____

_____

_____

_____

Loved me by:

_____

_____

_____

_____

Challenged me to:

_____

_____

_____

_____

Developed qualities in me like:

_____

_____

_____

_____

Made me laugh so hard when:

_____

_____

_____

_____

Reminded me of how awesome life is when:

_____

_____

_____

_____

Helped me rebound after I experienced:

_____

_____

_____

_____

Built my self-esteem by:

_____

_____

_____

_____

Showed me how strong I really am when:

_____

_____

_____

_____

Reminded me how special I am by:

_____

_____

_____

_____

Taught me the value of:

_____

_____

_____

_____

Left me with the responsibility to:

_____

_____

_____

_____

Would want me to carry out their legacy by:

_____

_____

_____

_____

Wow friend, I don't know about you, but after completing this simple yet powerful exercise, I personally feel a great deal of gratitude toward my loved one. I hope you feel the same. I know in my heart they would want you thriving through this loss in your life by being grateful for the many wonderful things you gained by having them in your life.

Originally, this chapter was not included in the final manuscript, but after experiencing this loss, I realized that I now had a completely new "storm" to write about. I pray that as you've read through this chapter, it has sparked some new healing in your mind, body, and soul. It is also my hope and prayer that you found comfort and support from the words on these pages.

I am truly sorry for your loss.

CHAPTER SUMMARY

✦ Remember: don't try to be strong. Be authentic with your feelings in the moment.

✦ Allow yourself to be fully supported during this time.

✦ Focus on your loved one's gain, rather than your loss.

✦ Send your loved one home to the best of your ability.

✦ Realize that you did the best you could.

✦ Believe you'll get stronger each day but will have "moments."

✦ Know that your loved one is truly in a better place.

✦ Create something that honors their life.

✦ Understand that the way you lived your life was your most lasting impression on them.

✦ Express gratitude for the amount of time you were blessed to have them in your life.

Massive Action Plan

Write down your action plan based on what you learned from this chapter.

_____

_____

_____

_____

_____

_____

PART TWO

The Components of Your Comeback

Know Your Value

7

YOU ARE SO MUCH MORE
THAN YOU REALIZE

The purpose of this chapter is to empower you on a topic I once needed help with myself, both personally and professionally, and that's *knowing your value*.

I'm so thankful that I've had great people for so long in my life to consistently reinforce me, because if you're going to thrive through your storms, you've got to know your value—that it's so much greater than the things you possess or the titles you hold.

When you understand that your *intrinsic* is always going to be far more valuable than your *extrinsic*, you begin to

> "When your value is clear, your decision is easy."
>
> —Jonas Gadson

thrive because you come to realize that your value doesn't diminish, but in fact actually grows to a higher level, based on what you grow through.

My corporation is called Platinum Performance Global, and we help organizations and individuals of all types not just *go* to the next level but *grow* to the next level. Ultimately, we enable them to see that their value doesn't change because of what happens to them. Society and the people around us—negative as well as positive, well-meaning people—often try to make us believe our value goes down as a direct result of our experiences. And I get why that happens; we've probably all been guilty of that mindset at one time or another.

To illustrate this point, let me ask you a question. Have you ever assumed: *Someone who has spent time in prison probably can't be successful now.* Sure, there may be a stigma attached to those who've been incarcerated, but what if I were to tell you that there are multimillionaires and top business owners in America who've done jail time? Let's face it: Even Martha Stewart found herself in that situation, and though it was a bit rocky at first, she not only regained but continued to grow her business success without much of a hitch.

✎ Can you think of any times in your life when a negative experience made you feel less valuable? If so, write down up to three. Indicate if a stigma remained with you long term due to these experiences, or if judgment of you by others faded rather quickly; then note if you have overcome, learned a vital lesson, and/ or become better because of the challenges.

_____

_____

_____

_____

_____

_____

_____

See, it's not so much what we *go* through but how we *grow* through it that makes us better. Your value isn't lessened because of difficulties; it actually gets higher because you conquered them. When you examine a list of super successful people and discover the things they've been through, it's really quite remarkable. I highly recommend Dr. John C Maxwell's book, *Failing Forward*, in which he explores the failure stories of some of the most successful people in the world. And because I know you may be experiencing what you believe is a failure in your life right now, I especially dedicate this next section to those whose value may feel diminished. Perhaps one or more of these scenarios hits home for you:

✦ You've been through a relationship change ...
You feel less valuable because you don't have the connection you once had.

✦ You've been through a career change ...
You feel less valuable because you don't have the important title you used to have.

✦ You used to be a VP of something ...
You feel less valuable because you lost a sense of importance.

✦ You had to stop taking classes ...
You feel less valuable because you can't afford to finish school right now.

✦ You're a parent and don't have the relationship you wish you had with your children ...
You feel less valuable because the strain between you and your spouse/ex is affecting your parenting.

✦ You don't have the fancy house you used to have ...
You feel less valuable because the economy caused you to downsize.

✦ The 401K you worked twenty, thirty, forty years to accumulate has dwindled ...
You feel less valuable because the declining market has decreased your funds.

Delatorro L. McNeal, II

✦ Your child in college has changed majors five times …
You feel less valuable because that tuition bill is sucking you dry.

✦ You don't have health insurance and bam! A health challenge hit your life …
You feel less valuable because you have to deal with astronomical medical expenses you weren't prepared for.

✦ You had to take a pay cut or were laid off …
You feel less valuable because you worked hard to maintain that position.

✦ You couldn't afford your payment and your car got repossessed …
You feel less valuable because you're now reliant on others or on public transportation.

If any of these challenges are familiar to you—and I know how painful they can be—I'm here to remind you that it doesn't matter what happens *to* you; what matters is what happens *inside* you. You still have tremendous value, and I hope this next example that I use in my keynotes all across the country and around the world will drive that message home.

No matter what type of organization or company I'm speaking to on the topic of personal value, the following illustration proves to be highly powerful:

I'll pull out, say, a fifty dollar bill and show it to the entire audience.

"What is this?" I ask.

"A fifty dollar bill," they say.

"How many of you in this room can think of things you can do with this fifty dollar bill right now?"

Of course, every hand goes up, and people start shouting the things they want to do with fifty dollars.

And so I ask: "How many of you would like to have it?"

Everybody's hand goes up. "Oh, me, me, me, me, me," the audience shrieks.

And so I say: "Ok, now what if I do this," and I begin to take my audience through a series of actions that would normally cause an object to lose its value. For example, I'll start by taking the fifty dollar bill and crumpling it up. Then I ask: "How many of you still want this fifty dollar bill?"

As expected, every hand goes up.

Then I'll throw the fifty dollar bill on the ground and start jumping up and down on it, doing anything I can to squash it. Then I pick it up and ask: "Now who wants this fifty dollar bill?"

Everybody still wants it.

Then I look at it and say: "You know what, you're nothing. You're only a fifty dollar bill. My debts are much bigger than you, fifty; I need way more than you. All you are is a fifty dollar bill and that's all you're ever going to be. You'll never be a hundred, two hundred, a thousand. The best you'll ever be is a fifty dollar bill." And I say all these things to decrease that bill's self-esteem and self-value. Then I ask the audience: "Who still wants this fifty dollar bill?"

Again, every hand goes up.

The interesting thing is, if I were to look at that fifty dollar bill and say: "You know what, I'm done with you. You don't meet my needs, my expectations, the things I want out of life, so I'm breaking up with you. I'm going to find me a hundred, or a thousand, or a million. And I break up with the fifty, hold it up to the audience, and say: "How many of you all *still* want this fifty dollar bill?"

You guessed it: *Everybody*.

My friend, no matter what I said to it, did to it, or how I treated it, that fifty dollar bill didn't change. No matter what external things I tried to do to negatively influence the internal value of it, I couldn't destroy its worth unless I literally took scissors and cut it up or burned it. I'd have to physically destroy it in order for it to lose its value.

Delatorro L. McNeal, II

In addition—and perhaps even more important—I'm here to tell you that that fifty dollar bill is still worth fifty dollars whether it's in my wallet or a Louis Vuitton wallet or a Guess wallet. In other words, it doesn't matter what's wrapped around it; it's still a fifty dollar bill, and it still has tremendous value. The same goes for your life. Ok, some of the things that were wrapped around it might now be gone. Any number of things may have your value feeling diminished:

✦ The economy	✦ Depression
✦ The unemployment rate	✦ The stock market
✦ The real estate market	✦ A lay off
✦ A failed relationship	✦ A bankruptcy
✦ A medical diagnosis	✦ A credit score issue
✦ A wayward family member	✦ A divorce
✦ Low self-esteem	✦ Fill in the blank

A storm has hit your life at some point, and because of it you've probably felt like you've lost your value. But, my friend, I want you to understand that you are far more valuable than anything that can ever happen to you. No matter how society paints it, what you can contribute to this world with your gifts and talents is much more valuable than the things you possess. Scripture reminds us that "greater is He that is within us than he that is in the world." In other words, what's in you is greater than what you're in.

We have the nerve to say things like: "Oh, I've lost everything." No, you haven't lost everything. There's still a whole lot you have left (and we're going to expound on that in a future chapter). But for now, I want you to understand that there is much more in you, that you're much more valuable than what you drive, what you wear, or the house you live in. With that firmly in your mind, I want you to do the following exercise:

List five <u>characteristics</u> you possess that make you valuable.

_____   _____

_____

_____

_____

_____

You see how those things have nothing to do with the material?

I remember one time I was at a speaking engagement and three young men came up to me.

"You're Mr. Success Man, ain't you? You're the man that's going to teach us to be successful and live our dreams."

"Absolutely," I said. "Are you all coming to the session?"

"Well, it kind of depends," one said. "We'll come only if you tell us first what kind of car you drive."

We were walking at the time and the question made me stop.

"What?"

"Yeah, Mr. Success Man, we'll come to your session only if we're satisfied with the answer you give us about what kind of car you drive."

Now I didn't have a problem answering the question because I drive a nice car, but in my mind I thought: _How sad…these young men are in the presence of another young man—who happens to be me—who is extremely successful, and they could learn some things from me if they just came and opened up their hearts and minds and ears, took great notes, and applied this information to their lives. But unfortunately, they're going to potentially miss out because they've got the meaning of success all wrong._

See, my friend, they were asking the wrong question.

> It doesn't matter what successful people drive;
> what matters is what drives successful people.

If you were to stop reading this book right now, this message alone would be worth what you paid for it. You see, those young men were so focused on the *extrinsic* that they didn't know it was the *intrinsic* that makes the extrinsic possible. If you deposit into your internal value, you can create anything external that you desire. That's why you can't let the loss of anything that happens to you on the outside decrease your value on the inside. To that end, I'm going to give you a list of statements, and I want you to confirm it by writing the words *I am* in each blank.

_____ much more valuable than a car.

_____ much more valuable than a house.

_____ much more valuable than a 401K statement.

_____ much more valuable than the person who left me.

_____ much more valuable than the job I just lost.

_____ much more valuable than the job I'm applying for right now.

_____ much more valuable than my current occupation will ever communicate to me.

_____ much more valuable than that gated community I can't afford to live in any longer.

_____ much more valuable than that fancy purse, man bag, or satchel I carry.

_____ much more valuable than the properties I might have lost in the real estate market.

_____ much more valuable than my bank accounts.

_____ much more valuable than the bill collectors try to make me out to be because I'm behind in my payment.

You see, crises and challenging times attempt to strip us of all the things that used to clothe us because we live in a society where everything is based on trend, fashion, style, and glitz; what you drive and where you live; what you do and where you shop; what kind of groceries you buy and whether you purchase name brands or generic. Relying on the physical things we use to identify ourselves makes it difficult when we lose them. And listen, I'm not talking from theory or books, I'm talking about things I've lived through in my own personal and professional life.

I know what it's like to have the big house and the small house, the super cool ride and the not so cool ride, a fat bank account and a not so fat bank account, tons of properties in my real estate portfolio and no properties at all. I've learned in all situations, as Scripture reminds us, to be content with what God has blessed me with. And I want to challenge and encourage you to do the same.

In order to thrive through your storm, you cannot be clothed by what money can get you. Yeah, it's great to have nice threads, nice rides, nice houses; there's nothing wrong with having nice things. There's simply something wrong with nice things having *you*. And if you use the accumulation of these nice things to clothe you, then guess what? When they're gone, you feel stark naked—empty and worthless. You feel unsuccessful, like an underachiever, like a failure. But I'm going to be different from a lot of those rah rah programs out there and tell you that that's ok. It's natural for you to feel like that because that's what you relied on to clothe you. So go ahead—embrace it; feel it. Just promise me you won't hold onto those feelings too long; they aren't the ones that make up who you truly are.

✎ List 3–5 material things you may have lost in your life that had/have you feeling down.

Now reflect on those things. Has that loss obliterated the characteristics you possess that you listed on page 79?

There have been times when I've written bestselling books but didn't feel like the person on the cover at that particular point in my life. There were times I had to get in front of thousands of people and inspire them to live their dreams when I felt like I was living my own nightmare. But one of the things I can honestly tell you is that it's ok in that moment to feel like a failure, to feel unsuccessful, because to feel otherwise would make you inhuman. And no matter what we deal with, my friend, we're all human beings.

So it's ok to feel naked because you lost some stuff. But I want to encourage you by telling you that none of those things you lost brought value to you. The truth is, *you* brought value to *them*. Here's what I mean by that.

Let's just say that you lost the nice house you once had. Let me ask you this: Was it the house that made you more valuable, fulfilled, or happier, or was it your spirit, your vitality, your energy, your smile, your flair for decorating, your good taste, and/or your hospitality that brought value to that house? Yes, that structure was tangible and meant something to you, but when you think about it, you'll see it was *you* who brought value to it. And if you can bring value and life to that house, guess what? You can bring it to another.

Now it's important here that you don't get this message twisted. Not everybody who drives a nice car is happy inside. It's one thing to have the wrapping of a nice car, but guess what? I'd rather be in a Pinto with the woman of my dreams than be in a big fat Hummer and be miserable with the person I'm sharing my life with. I'd rather have the internal things right than have the wrapping that portrays life being "right" to the world when it's really horribly wrong. Because the truth is, what you really want is both.

> You want the intrinsic to be right and the extrinsic to match it.

So go ahead and create a vision board, see the things that you want, and begin to take the action necessary to obtain—or re-obtain—the items that make you feel good. Because nice clothes, a nice watch, nice shoes— all these things *do* make you feel good, and there's nothing wrong with that as long as it *adds* to you and doesn't *make* you.

My friend, remember how no matter what I did to that fifty dollar bill, everybody in the audience still wanted it? Why? Because they understood its intrinsic value. And if that mindset can work for a bill, what about for you?

✦ What about the gifts, talents, skills, and resources that are in you? *Doesn't that have value?*

✦ What about all the people you've helped at one time or another? *Doesn't that have value?*

✦ What about all the books you've read? *Doesn't that have value?*

✦ What about all the memories you have up to this point in your life? *Don't they have value?*

✦ What about the smiles from those who love you and the friends and colleagues who treasure who you are? *Doesn't that have tremendous value?*

✦ What about all the people you've served and for whom you've paid it forward? *Doesn't that have value?*

✦ What about the life lessons you've learned and the wisdom you've gained throughout it all? *Doesn't that have value?*

✦ Doesn't your personality, your disposition, who you are in this thing called life, have value?

Absolutely it does.

My friend, know your value. And when you do, as my good buddy Jonas Gadson says: "When your value is clear, the decision is easy."

Delatorro L. McNeal, II

CHAPTER SUMMARY

Though it may be one of life's biggest challenges to recognize your value when you've lost material things or are feeling like you've failed at something—even when you had no control over the situation—it's vital for you to know that your value has nothing to do with the extrinsic (outside) and everything to do with the intrinsic (inside). To that end, I want you to reflect on:

✦ How you've overcome and learned from negative experiences in your life

✦ The internal characteristics you possess that make you valuable

✦ The material things you may have lost but that haven't robbed you of your true worth

Massive Action Plan

Write down your action plan based on what you learned from this chapter.

_____

_____

_____

_____

_____

_____

Ask Yourself Better Questions

8

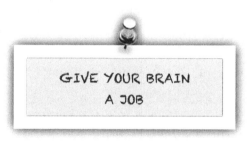

GIVE YOUR BRAIN
A JOB

I'm convinced there's nothing that happens to us in life that makes us ask more questions than difficult times. Think about it: When something great occurs, you might pinch yourself and say: "Is this really happening to me?" But you accept it; you say things like: "Cool!" "This is awesome!" "I love it!" "How wonderful!" You don't doubt or second guess it. But oh, my friend, nothing makes us stew, doubt, cross-examine, or prosecute ourselves more than when we go through challenging times. Because at the end of the day, what are we trying to do? We're trying to understand.

See, when something good happens, it's like: "Ok, great! I'll understand it later; let me just enjoy it now." But when it's something bad, you strive to understand what's going on emotionally, physically, financially, psychologically, relationally, occupationally, and even spiritually. And so as you're trying to make sense out of chaos and comprehend why bad things happen to good, hardworking, praying, loving, giving, sharing, serving, volunteering, tithing people, the natural cognitive reaction is to question. Now, here's the problem with that: Most people tend to ask bad questions.

Let me teach you something about the way your brain works. It may be obvious, but here it is: Your brain is going to answer whatever question you ask it, and it will do so within the same tone, vernacular, or disposition in which you asked.

> "The quality of the answers you get in your life are determined by the quality of questions that you ask."
>
> —Tony Robbins

For example: If you ask yourself a question with good energy, you're going to get an answer with good energy back. Your brain is a mirror, and it gives back whatever you're projecting. So if you ask yourself negative questions with a bad, disempowering state of being, you're going to get bad, negative, disempowering answers. So, my friend, as a part of my commitment to help you thrive through your storm, I'm going to teach you how to ask yourself better questions.

Have you ever realized the scope of what you ask when times are tough? You tend to question:

+ Your life
+ God
+ Your situation
+ Your past, present & future

+ Your dreams
+ Your gifts, talents, abilities, and skills
+ Yourself

What you may not realize, however, is that the better the question we ask, the better the answer. So since we're not all aware of how to implement that practice, I'm going to share with you ten questions to ask yourself when you're going through tough circumstances in life. When something's not working out the way you planned, hoped, or expected, these questions offer powerful, productive, purposeful means to help you thrive through your storm.

Before I give these to you, though, you have an important assignment. You must promise to stop asking the bad questions, such as:

- ✦ "What did I do to deserve this?"
- ✦ "Why did this have to happen to me?"
- ✦ "Why is life so unfair?"

- ✦ "Why is God mad at me?"
- ✦ "Why don't things ever work out for me?"
- ✦ "Why am I so stupid?"

You promise? Ok. Let's move on to much better ways of reflecting on your circumstance so you can become a champion of overcoming and learning.

QUESTION #1

Why was I chosen to learn from this experience?

What does this question do? It automatically phrases the end result of your situation in the positive. Anything you learn from is no longer a failure; it's a life lesson. And the *why was I chosen* part? That's powerful too because you have to understand that sometimes you've been trusted with trouble and chosen for challenge. For example:

> Why would God or life choose you to go through something difficult? Maybe because they know you have a big mouth, and once you've gone through your challenge, you're going to tell other people to help liberate them. So maybe the reason is to help other people.

> No matter what, there's a purpose behind your being chosen.

✎ Consider a challenge you recently had and use it for each of the following exercises. Why do you think you were chosen to learn from this experience?

Delatorro L. McNeal, II

QUESTION #2

Who is in my life—or who will come into my life—that I can bless or help as a result of what I'm learning in this experience?

My friend, everything you're going through is teaching you something—there's no better teacher than life itself. In fact, I double-dog-dare you to dig the lesson out of your current challenge. Because if you can do that, you can pass it on to someone else, and you never know the impact that could have on their life.

✎ Who is in your life, or has come into your life, that you've been able to bless from the lesson you've learned? How?

_____

_____

_____

_____

QUESTION #3

How will I be better because of this?

It's so important to understand that problems come into your life to make you *better*, but we often choose to allow them to make us *bitter*, and that's not what they were designed to do.

Every single successful person goes through challenging times, and it's in those times that they improve. It's the same for you. Take comfort in knowing there's a blessing on the other side of this, that there are people waiting to learn from you and be inspired by the fact that you made it out of whatever challenge tackled you. I know it might not make sense right now, and I get that you may be asking:

- ✦ "How am I going to be better when I've lost all my money?"
- ✦ "How am I going to be better when I've lost my credit?"
- ✦ "How am I going to be better when I've lost my house?"
- ✦ "How am I going to be better, Del? I don't see it."

I know how you're feeling—been there, done that, got the t-shirt and the keychain. My friend, just hang on; it's going to be all right. Trust me. You might not feel it today, tomorrow, or even next week, but you're going to be better because of this, I promise.

✒ How have you become better through your challenging situation?

_____

_____

_____

_____

_____

QUESTION #4

Did this need to happen to make me a better person for something that's coming in my future?

Think about that. I believe that oftentimes we don't change in life until something shakes us and gives us no other choice. Because we're creatures of habit, we get comfortable. We get too complacent with life the way it is, and for our future to really manifest itself into our present, we have to be shaken. Sometimes we've got to shed the old skin of an aspect of our lives to make room for the new; it can't find its place if we're cluttered by junk that doesn't belong there anymore. It's your responsibility to recognize that and to make a way for the new opportunity.

Delatorro L. McNeal, II

What is life trying to get you to do that you wouldn't have done if things didn't get challenging?

QUESTION #5

Whose hurt can I now identify with because I've been through this?

Isn't it amazing how often we view a particular circumstance one way until it happens to us? Think about the following:

We can be pretty cocky as parents when our kids are doing well, and when you hear about a child who's not doing well, you say: "Oh, at least my son or daughter doesn't do that." And you have that little arrogant kind of self-righteousness about you in your parenting skills until your child acts a fool, and then all of a sudden, that arrogance is dashed; you now can relate to that parent who raised their child well, but he or she just took a wrong turn.

Perhaps you can likewise relate to the person who did their best on the job but still got laid off—and it wasn't because of the lack of performance … or the person who's been unemployed for months despite their best efforts to find work. Or what about how easy it is to be snobbish about your relationship or your marriage and look down on other people who are separated or divorced, thinking: "Oh, that would never happen to me." But it's striking how the tune changes when you find yourself going through the same or similar situation.

See, tough times often come to sensitize our hearts to the issues of others. Because when you've been through it, you have a tender heart toward those who experience the same heartache. When you've been abused, you have a tender heart toward those who've also been abused. When you've had to live in your car, you have a tender heart toward those who are homeless. When you've been hungry, you have a tender heart toward those who don't have groceries. There's a lot to be said for the ability to appreciate others' adversity and to understand another's pain.

🖎 Whose hurt can you identify with because of your situation? Name some types of people you can now relate to.

_____

_____

_____

_____

_____

QUESTION #6

How can I begin again?

It's not unusual for us in tough times to say: "It's over … I'm done … I can't do it … I can't make it." But when you start the question off with "how" and change the words slightly, your brain suddenly gets working.

One of my greatest friends is Traci Bild—an incredible sales trainer, bestselling author, and entrepreneur—and she says something that I love, love, love:

> "Your brain wants a job, so give it the job of doing what you want it to do."

If you say, for example: "I can't afford it," your brain doesn't have a job. Why? Because you just told your brain: *Don't think. Don't process. Don't function. Don't be creative. Don't be innovative. Just shut down.* But when you shift the question to: *How can I afford that?*, you've given your brain a job. Now it can launch like a missile and begin to seek out ways to make something happen for you so that you can afford anything you wish.

Don't leave your brain sitting there on the sidelines; get it in the game, my friend. Ask yourself how you can begin again with:

- ✦ The credit you have left
- ✦ The money you have left
- ✦ The property you have left
- ✦ The friends you have left
- ✦ The reputation you have left
- ✦ The skills, talents, and abilities you have left

✎ With whatever you have left, how can you begin again?

_____

_____

_____

_____

_____

QUESTION #7

Who am I really?

Oh, I love this question. See, challenging times disturb a lot of the stuff you use to define who you are and attack the things you use to clothe yourself, such as:

<table>
<tr><td>✦ Your house</td><td>✦ Your wardrobe</td></tr>
<tr><td>✦ Your possessions</td><td>✦ Your kids</td></tr>
<tr><td>✦ Your car</td><td>✦ Your family</td></tr>
<tr><td>✦ Your credit</td><td>✦ Your belief in God</td></tr>
<tr><td>✦ Your friendships</td><td>✦ Your belief in yourself</td></tr>
<tr><td>✦ Your reputation</td><td>✦ Your self-esteem</td></tr>
<tr><td>✦ The way people see you</td><td>✦ Your self-worth</td></tr>
<tr><td>✦ Your finances</td><td>✦ Your self-confidence</td></tr>
</table>

All of these things get called into question when you go through troublesome times. So a great question to ask yourself is: *With all of that stuff gone, who am I?*

Are you still beautiful? *Yes.*

Are you still handsome? *Absolutely.*

Are you still brilliant? *Yes.*

Are you still smart as a whip? *Absolutely.*

Are you still a creative genius? *Yes.*

Do you still have gifts, talents, abilities, and skills that this world has not even begun to see at their fullest potential? *Yes.*

You're made in the image and likeness of God, which means you are an incredible human being. See, life may give us a bunch of titles—spouse, business owner, "top five percent," homeowner, etc.—but sometimes challenging times strip us of some of those titles. So once you no longer claim what you identified yourself with, who are you really?

I'm here to tell you that you're still *you.* You're still beautiful. You're still smart. You're still wise. You're still gifted and talented. You're still amazing.

Delatorro L. McNeal, II

✎ Who are you really after what you lost was stripped away?

_____

_____

_____

_____

QUESTION #8

How can I profit from this pain that I'm experiencing?

My friend, the reason I love this question is because once again, it makes your brain go to work. When you ask how you can somehow reap reward from the burden you're going through right now, you realize you can benefit by:

+ Teaching other people
+ Encouraging other people
+ Journaling your progress and process
+ Speaking about it
+ Doing workshops that help other people
+ Becoming a spokesperson for groups of people who have dealt with the same issue(s)

Here's a powerful example:

You were in a car accident where the person who hit you and caused the accident was drinking and driving, and someone dear to you died. You survived … and so did the drunk driver. Now, it's only natural that you would say: "How in the world can I profit from this pain?" Many times profit is not financial or even related to money; it can signify the ability you possess to turn a tragedy around for the good. And you may choose to do that by traveling across the country and sharing your story in order to teach other people about the dangers of drunk driving, encouraging people to make better choices and be smarter when they drive.

✎ Write down a way you can profit, either financially or otherwise, from the difficulty you've faced.

_____

_____

_____

_____

QUESTION #9

What lessons have I learned that will help me make better decisions moving forward?

Tough times, my friend, are just like classes in school—you only want to take them once. You strive to learn the lesson and then graduate. Think about it: Who wants to be in the fifth grade five times? … or the eighth grade six times? … or a college freshman five times in a row? Nobody. You want to experience that level and then move forward.

✎ How can you now make better decisions moving forward from the lesson you've learned?

_____

_____

_____

_____

Delatorro L. McNeal, II

QUESTION #10

What do I need to do, create, start, or build to give voice to this experience in order to bless others and myself?

Here are some ways you can foster connections with others who may value your support:

✦ Create a group on LinkedIn

✦ Establish a fan page on FaceBook

✦ Begin a group on Meetup.com

✦ Start a cell group at your place of worship

✦ Build a network or website

✦ Write a book

✦ Host a workshop

✦ Volunteer

Bottom line: Realize there are numerous ways to rally together and give a voice to your experience. For a compelling example, look at the origins of MADD:

> Mothers got tired of losing their children in drunk driving accidents, so they came together and started Mothers Against Drunk Driving to be a support for one another, give voice to the issue and the cause, love one another, help each other through the challenging times, and strive to keep more moms from losing their children.

✎ Which of the above list are you willing to commit to in order to give voice to your experience?

_____

_____

_____

BONUS QUESTION #1

Is there anything that I can be grateful for?

My friend, I want you to ask yourself right now if there's anything in your life, in spite of what's going on, that you can be grateful for. What about the simple fact that you can read this book? Or the meal you had today? Or the fact that you're breathing right now?

One of the things that's going to turn your situation around the quickest is *gratitude*. The more you wake up every day with an attitude of gratitude and make a mental or physical list of the things you're grateful for—in spite of what may not be going the way you want—you're going to come out of your storm faster, I guarantee it.

✎ Though I asked you to do this in Chapter 3, I want you to write down at least ten things you're grateful for in your life right now, but this time, focus on your challenging situation.

_____

_____

_____

_____

_____

_____

_____

_____

_____

_____

_____

_____

BONUS QUESTION #2

What am I proud of?

In spite of the successes you've had, you may very well be experiencing one of the following situations:

+ You're going through a test.
+ You believe life isn't fair right now.
+ You have more bills than money.
+ Your relationship is on the rocks.
+ Your reputation is kind of wavering.
+ You've made some bad decisions.
+ You were supposed to learn from something but didn't, and so you fell into a similar situation yet again.
+ Your job isn't what you want it to be.
+ Your business is struggling.
+ You feel miles away from God.
+ You believe your prayers aren't being answered.
+ You don't understand where your life is going.
+ You feel like you can never make enough money.

But in the face of one or more of these challenges, I want you to ask yourself what you're proud of. Do you feel how that shifts the atmosphere? Your list will be unique to you, of course, but here are a few of mine:

+ I'm proud of the fact that I got my degree(s).
+ I'm proud that the people in my life love me.
+ I'm proud that I've done my best throughout my career.
+ I'm proud that I care and enjoy helping others whenever I can.
+ I'm proud that I've survived some of my darkest moments.

What do you have to be proud of?

_____

_____

_____

_____

_____

_____

_____

_____

_____

_____

_____

My friend, I urge you to take these twelve powerful, forward thinking, creative, innovative questions and apply them in your life right now so that you can get better answers. Remember: The quality of answers you get are determined by the quality of questions you ask. Start asking yourself better questions, and you really will get better answers. Give your brain something to do other than worry and stress and fret and be afraid. Give it a job, and it's going to produce for you.

No matter what happens ...

ASK BETTER QUESTIONS.

CHAPTER SUMMARY

We're so conditioned in our society to ask *Why me?* when things are bad, yet we're usually focused on the negative side and rarely concentrate on the good that underlies the difficulty. I want to turn that way of thinking upside-down for you—because I guarantee that you, and your life, will change for the better once you do. To that end, I challenge you to shift your attention to the following when times are rough:

✦ Know the reason you were chosen is to learn and grow from the experience.

✦ Believe you will be a better person and a great resource for others.

✦ See the tough times as helping you become less judgmental and more compassionate.

✦ Trust you have the internal resources to begin again if necessary.

✦ Understand that there is opportunity for profit from every hardship.

✦ Embrace gratitude for what you still have, even in the face of adversity.

Massive Action Plan

Write down your action plan based on what you learned from this chapter.

_____

_____

_____

_____

_____

Keep Driving the Bus

9

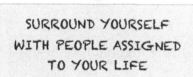

SURROUND YOURSELF
WITH PEOPLE ASSIGNED
TO YOUR LIFE

Have you ever been through a trial in your life, and while you were going through it—as if the test wasn't bad enough by itself—you ended up losing friends at the same time?

When friendships cease with those you believed would be there for you —friends into whom you deposited so much time, supported, and believed that when your turn came, they would surely be on your side—it's incredibly painful. It's as if they stuck a knife into you and twisted it, then pulled it out and threw salt on the wound.

My friends, I know what it's like—and I know *you* know what it's like— to lose friends in the storm. But I want to encourage you in this chapter to keep driving the bus.

People come into our lives for a reason, a season, and some—in fact very few—for a lifetime. It's imperative that you understand the distinct types of friends you have and the varied purposes of those relationships in your life in different seasons. This way you can adjust your expectations.

One of the things that makes the whole notion of friendships so murky is the social media-driven society we live in today. And listen, I'm thankful for social media; I love it and think it's a really cool thing. However, I truly believe that as a society we've almost completely lost what it means to have true, genuine friends. Why? Partly because the word *friend* has become an all-encompassing term. Your number of friends can now mean:

+ a calculation of the total number of individuals you have in your social media profile
+ how many Facebook friends, fans, and likes you have
+ how many followers you have on Twitter
+ how many connections you have on LinkedIn
+ how many followers you have on your blog
+ how many people you have on your mailing list, many of whom you don't even know

But I want you to understand something. You can have hundreds or thousands from the above list, but isn't it amazing how when you go through a really tough time—when life hits you with something you didn't expect, and the things that mean a lot to you start to get shaken—you'd be lucky to have five people you could truly count on and call real friends.

See, all of that social media stuff is wonderful, but at the end of the day you need people in your life who are there—period. You don't need fair weather friends or shady chums; you don't need folks who are only there for you when things are going well. You need rocks, people who are roots to your tree. True friends are those who are there for you in, out, up, down, no matter what. They're the ones who've got your back, but they're also sometimes going to:

- ✦ disagree with you
- ✦ correct you
- ✦ tell you that your opinion is a bad one
- ✦ tell you that your attitude stinks

But even in the face of those things, Scripture reminds us: "Faithful are the wounds of a friend." In other words, if a friend says something to you and it kind of hurts a little bit, the "faithful" part signifies that their heart was in the right place. Their words might have stung you, but they only said them because they believed they were true and would help you grow as a person. *Quality*, not *quantity*, is the objective of friendships.

I want to be honest with you: When you go through storms in your life and lose some friends in the process, the reality is that it hurts, it sucks, it's embarrassing, it's painful ... but it's life. When you experience some of the gut-wrenching situations that surround you, not every person you consider a friend is going to stick by you.

I am truly fortunate to not only have an incredible network of friends, mentors, and family, but I've been blessed to be in a circle of very successful people, and I know the wealthiest of the wealthy and the broke of the broke. The commonality among the varied socioeconomic statuses of people I have relationships with is that each of them has lost at least one friend when they've gone through tough times. That's why I dedicated an entire chapter to this topic, to give you a strategy and to help you deal with this loss when you weather the storms of your life.

> I truly believe that understanding is the key to withstanding.

If you can understand what's going on and why, it gives you a better ability to withstand what you're going through. To that end, I want to share why not every friend will be with you for the long haul.

Delatorro L. McNeal, II

REASON #1

Everybody who's *with* you is not *for* you.

Whether you realize it or not, you've been in a business from the time you were born. What business, you ask? The business of people management. Every single day you've had people crossing your path—some as a brief encounter, some remaining for a long time, some straddling the fence of staying in or out, and some leaving. We're constantly surrounded by people. But the key to keep in mind is this: Not everyone who's *with* you is *for* you. This applies to all areas of your life:

✦ Those walking in your circle

✦ Those in your business

✦ Those in your family

✦ Those at your job

Likewise, when it comes to your dream, not everyone will support you; when it comes to success, not everyone will be happy for you. Why? Because people who are *with* you tend to stay with you as long as things are good. But those who are *for* you will go further than that. They:

✦ fight for you   ✦ come up with ideas for you

✦ pray for you   ✦ mastermind for you

✦ believe in you   ✦ volunteer for you

✦ have faith in you   ✦ serve for you

✦ raise money for you   ✦ brainstorm for you

✦ cook for you   ✦ are creative for you

✦ support you

You get what I'm saying? Everybody who's *with* you, my friend, is not *for* you.

REASON #2

Many people in your life are connected to your *success* not to your *life*.

People can sometimes leave your life easily because they were aligned with you only as long as:

- ✦ things were going well
- ✦ you were popular
- ✦ you were in the media and getting good press
- ✦ you could do things for them
- ✦ knowing you was beneficial for them
- ✦ you introduced them to people they wouldn't otherwise meet
- ✦ you hooked them up with some credibility and/or status
- ✦ you could take them on nice trips with you
- ✦ you took them out on your boat or in your car
- ✦ you invited them over to your nice fancy house
- ✦ you provided for them

They were aligned with your success, not your journey, your anointing, your gifts, or your purpose. With that in mind, you have to be grateful for storms because they sometimes come to shift your perspective and sift the excess out of your life.

Here's an example: If you cook, you know that when you're finished boiling spaghetti, you pour that big pot of water and noodles into a strainer. After the water drains, you take the noodles, add them to the sauce, and mix it all together for a great spaghetti dinner. That strainer gets rid of the excess and only holds onto what's absolutely necessary. And that's what storms do; they rid us of excess—material things, routines, and yes, people. Those who are really only *with* you but not *for* you don't deserve a place in your life, but we don't always recognize that on our own.

Delatorro L. McNeal, II

> "If people can just get up, grab their stuff and walk out of your life, let them go; you don't need them. If they can leave that easily, they were not part of your long-term plans."
> —Bishop T.D. Jakes

Just like characters in a movie or play, certain people in your world are part of the beginning, some the middle, and others the end. Some only make a cameo appearance in one phase of your life and that's it. Yet we often try to hold onto them, not realizing their stay was meant to be brief. So don't try to grasp onto friendships and relationships when people are trying to go or when you know it's best to let them go—just keep driving the bus. Remember: A lot of people are aligned with your *success*, but only a few are aligned with your *life*.

✎ Write down four people who were in your life for a brief time that you thought would stay longer, four who've been with you for a long time, and four you believe will be in your life indefinitely.

Brief:

_____

_____

_____

_____

Long Time:

_____

_____

_____

_____

Indefinitely:

_____

_____

_____

_____

One of the things I believe will help you tremendously is learning how to categorize your relationships and friendships so that you can adjust your expectations. See, if you put the same level of expectation into every type of friendship, you're going to be quickly disappointed, especially by anyone who decides to leave your life.

Because it's bound to happen at some point, you need to understand that when certain people choose to exit, you need to let them go. Why? Because God never closes one door without opening another. If a negative person leaves your life, He allows for a new, quality relationship to come in. So don't hold onto toxic people who really aren't *for* you but are merely connected to your success.

"But what if they're good people?" you ask. Just imagine that their stop has come and it's time for them to get off. And after the doors close and they walk away, I want you to keep driving the bus; after all, there are different types of friendships you'll encounter throughout your life.

#1: COMMON PLACE FRIENDSHIPS

These are people you consistently see in a familiar place and therefore develop a friendship. You may see them:

+ at the gym
+ at work
+ at church

+ at the park
+ in the neighborhood
+ at networking functions

In truth, they are likely more of an acquaintance or associate, but we call them friends because of the frequency with which we see them. You have no real connection with these types of friends; rather, you know only surface information about them. You may enjoy talking to them when you see them, but you wouldn't really miss them if they were gone.

Delatorro L. McNeal, II

✒ Name five Common Place Friendships in your life:

_____

_____

_____

_____

_____

#2: COMMON INTEREST FRIENDSHIPS

These are people with whom you share a specific hobby or pastime, such as:

- ✦ martial arts
- ✦ golf
- ✦ nonprofit involvement
- ✦ fashion

- ✦ ministry
- ✦ politics
- ✦ saving the world
- ✦ chess

These people may know a bit more about you than the common place friends, and you find you notice their absence and may even miss them when they're not there. Your common interest motivates you to call them friends.

✒ Name five Common Interest Friendships in your life:

_____

_____

_____

_____

_____

#3: COMMON CHALLENGE FRIENDSHIPS

These are people with whom you've gone through a similar challenge, such as:

+ being laid off from a job at the same time
+ single parenthood
+ graduating with the same degree and struggling to find a job
+ being friends as couples then both divorcing
+ going to AA together or being diagnosed with the same illness

Your common challenge creates a bond between you and can evolve into a stronger friendship. As I've stated before, trials make us sensitive to others who are experiencing similar challenges, so these connections can be quite meaningful.

Name five Common Challenge Friendships in your life:

_____

_____

_____

_____

_____

#4: COMMON PAST FRIENDSHIPS

These relationships are established due to similar backgrounds, such as:

+ growing up in the same neighborhood
+ attending the same high school or college
+ playing the same sports in the past

✦ your parents were friends in your youth

✦ taking music/art/dance lessons together

We often let these folks stay in our life just because we've known them for many years, but it's not unusual to outgrow them. Just because we've been connected for a long time doesn't mean they merit being called a real friend now. Remember: People come into our lives for a reason, a season, and some—in fact, very few—for a lifetime.

Name five Common Past Friendships in your life:

_____

_____

_____

_____

_____

#5: COMMON PROFESSION FRIENDSHIPS

It's not uncommon to befriend people in your same occupation. Whether you're both attorneys, doctors, entrepreneurs, real estate agents, philanthropists, engineers, or the like, your same line of work creates an automatic common bond.

Name five Common Profession Friendships in your life:

_____

_____

_____

_____

_____

Now there's nothing wrong with *common place* friends, *common interest* friends, *common challenge* friends, *common past* friends, or *common profession* friends, but it's vital not to let those surface commonalities make you think that person is a tried and true friend when they really aren't. What makes a person go from these friendship levels to the status of true friend is weathering challenging times.

You see, when someone's been through tough situations with you, they've seen you at the high and the low, with money and without, with popularity and without, etc. And they might not have agreed with all of your decisions, but they support you and love you, and they'll pray with you and ultimately want to see you thrive through your storm.

> A relationship that has not been tested cannot be trusted.

The problem with some common-level friendships is that the relationship never really gets tested. Think about how most everything we buy gets assessed for quality, yet we don't tend to let the people in our lives go through such tests before we trust them with our heart, our money, our stories, our business. So when they get up and leave, it hurts because you've trusted a source that was never tested.

See, when we were dropped on this earth, God gave us an assignment: Equipping us with gifts, talents, abilities, and skills, He gave us each a destination that He wanted us to head in. Throughout that journey, we're in the driver's seat of the bus called My Life Incorporated, and we've got room for all kinds of passengers. So as we go through life, people get on and off the bus. And guess what? We, as the bus drivers, need to not be swayed by those who leave, knowing not everyone was meant to stay on for the entire journey.

So my challenge to you is to be ok with the fact that certain people choose a particular time, avenue, lane, or boulevard to get off. But the beautiful part is that when folks get off, you just keep driving the bus. Because in a few lights, in a few blocks, in a few miles, some more people

Delatorro L. McNeal, II

are going to get on. Some more quality friends, mentors, couples, and business associates are going to come, believe me.

My friend, nothing and no one exits your life without something better coming to replace it. So while I'm sorry for the relationships you may have lost as you went through your storm, I'm thankful for and excited about the new ones that are on the way, because they're going to be phenomenal; the best is yet to come. Yeah, it hurts when some folks get off that you really counted on to stay on the ride with you, but guess what? When it hurts, you can pull over to the side, take a nap, get something to eat, and even mourn the loss; but then I want you to get back in the driver's seat, get on the intercom, and say:

"Ladies and gentlemen, this is (your name), and I'm the driver of this bus, and this bus is heading toward incredible success and significance, toward tremendous dreams. Anybody who feels the need to exit, please leave at this time. Those who are here for the journey, please stay on board."

Then I want you to turn on some good music, get people snapping their fingers, dancing, and smiling, and I want you to **keep driving the bus**.

CHAPTER SUMMARY

We may call numerous people *friends* in our lives, but the reality is that very few deserve the title of *true friend*. The challenging times we experience allow friendships to be tested, and the ones who aren't meant to stay with you for the long haul often fall by the wayside. The important thing is not to despair these losses too much; embrace the season they were with you and realize there are several types of friendships, some—but certainly not all—of which will result in lifelong connections:

✦ Those that stem from meeting often in a familiar place

✦ Those that are a result of a common interest

✦ Those born of experiencing a common challenge

✦ Those that flow from having a similar background

✦ Those that arise from sharing a work environment

Remember: Everybody who's *with* you is not necessarily *for* you; it's your responsibility to recognize the difference and celebrate the blessings of those who are your tried and true friends.

Massive Action Plan

Write down your action plan based on what you learned from this chapter.

_____

_____

_____

_____

_____

Delatorro L. McNeal, II

I Am the Shark

THRIVING
THROUGH
YOUR
STORMS

10

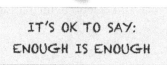

IT'S OK TO SAY:
ENOUGH IS ENOUGH

I was once at the community swimming pool with my daughters teaching Hope, my youngest, how to swim and find things underwater, while Miracle, my oldest, was playing with a boy named Carlos. Now Miracle was only five and in the shallow end with her little *floaties*, and Carlos, who was probably about a year older, was much more advanced in swimming than Miracle was. He was doing all these fancy tricks in the water, kind of showing off, when he decided to start playing this game with her called, "I Am the Shark."

He said: "Ok, I'm the shark, so anytime I growl and start splashing you, you have to try to get away." And he began making scary sounds and going after her, and she would run and swim fast to try to get away from him. Then he'd catch up to her and pretend to attack her by splashing water on her, and she would again try to swim or run and get out of the pool. This went on for about twenty minutes as I watched this young boy intimidating and kind of scaring my daughter in a playful way.

What I found interesting was that although they were having fun as kids, Miracle was truly in the position of the victim. She was constantly being attacked, the one who was always afraid and thrashing around in the water. Carlos was having a great time being the shark in the offensive position while Miracle was on the defensive. So as a dad, I finally decided I couldn't take it anymore and pulled Miracle to the side.

"Who said Carlos is the only one who could be The Shark?" I asked.

She shrugged.

"Ok. I want you to swim up to him," I said, "look him dead in his face and tell him: 'Carlos, I am the shark,' and then I want you to go after him, just like I taught you how to go after life, like when you fall off that bicycle, I tell you not to worry about falling down, to just get back up again and keep on pedaling. I want you to go after him like you go after that, and watch what happens."

So Miracle swam up to him, and with passion and determination, she said: "Carlos, I am the shark," and she started going after him. I'm telling you, that boy went ballistic. He was screaming and splashing, yelling "No, no, no, no. Stop chasing me. Stop, stop. Stop splashing me, stop swimming after me!" This boy, who had terrorized my daughter for nearly half an hour was now screaming at the top of his lungs in fear because Miracle had taken her power back and he was no longer the shark.

I'm telling you this story not just to give you a chuckle, but to help you understand that if you're going to thrive through your storm, every now and again you've got to let a little bit of healthy aggression rise up within you to where you say:

You know what? I'm not going to be the victim anymore. I'm not going to be the attacked anymore. I'm not going to be the one on the receiving end anymore. I'm not going to be on the defensive anymore. Starting today, I am the shark. I'm going to go after life, my problems, my enemy. I'm going to chase my storm rather than allow it to chase me. I deserve better than this. I'm worth more than this.

Delatorro L. McNeal, II

My friend, if you get that tenacity, that grit, that fortitude down in your belly and say, "Enough is enough," you'll be surprised by how empowered you feel and start to act.

Remember when you were a kid and you used to tease your friends about their clothes or music or lunch box or friends, but the one thing you couldn't poke fun at was someone's mama? Doing so meant you went a little too far, and that level of passion and anger would rear up in your friend and it was like, "Oh no, you done crossed the line."

My friend, I want you to get that kind of determination within you today—as circumstances are challenging you—to stand up to whatever's been attacking and frustrating you and reclaim your power. So wherever you are right now, if you're able, I want you to scream: "I am the shark!" If you can't scream it, I want you to say it within yourself, and do it with determination, passion, and drive, believing you can be in charge of your destiny. Don't sit there and wallow, crying *woe is me*. You've got to get up and make something happen.

A brilliant example is that of Rosa Parks. She got sick and tired of being sent to the back of the bus and said: "You know what? I am the shark. I'm going to sit in the front of the bus." Because of that inner strength and belief in what she deserved, she started a civil rights movement that has affected our world to this day.

Now while your trial may not spurn an advance that will change human history, perhaps you've been drained mentally, emotionally, and/or physically by:

- ✦ interviewing for countless jobs
- ✦ striving to pay those bills off
- ✦ attempting to work things out in a relationship
- ✦ trying to salvage a wavering friendship
- ✦ struggling to get your business off the ground
- ✦ vying for a promotion
- ✦ languishing in a family feud
- ✦ feeling beaten down by imposed expectations

In what areas of your life right now do you need to get some fortitude, some grit, some fight in you?

_____

_____

_____

_____

_____

_____

_____

Whatever you may be grappling with, if you've consistently been on the defensive, I want you to know that the ball is now in your hands, which means you're the offense, that you have the opportunity and the ability to score. But you can't win without getting in the driver's seat and taking control. You must do all you can to impact your situation and change your circumstance.

Remember, my friend, you cannot be who you want to be and be who you currently are at the same time. In order to shift from one to the other, you've got to proclaim: "I Am the Shark!"

CHAPTER SUMMARY

No one can really hold us back or down—only we can do that to ourselves. But until we realize that we must reclaim our power to effect change in our own lives, we will remain stagnant, frustrated, and likely defeated. To be "the shark" doesn't mean we intimidate or lord over others; rather, it signifies redeeming the strength and belief we may have lost while in a storm. You must believe that you have the prerogative and ability to:

✦ assert yourself if you feel taken for granted

✦ refuse to be a victim

✦ claim the respect you deserve

✦ declare your worth to yourself and others through your actions

✦ stand up for your rights as a human being

Massive Action Plan

Write down your action plan based on what you learned from this chapter.

_____

_____

_____

_____

_____

_____

_____

Make Lemonade and Sell It for Profit

11

DIFFICULTIES ARE
OPPORTUNITIES
IN DISGUISE

Let's talk candidly about exactly what it means to make lemonade and sell it for profit—or rather, about shifting your perspective so you can stop thinking *problem* and start thinking *profit*.

We've all heard: "When life hands you lemons, make lemonade." Now, I think that's great, but in order to truly capitalize on all you've been through, you've got to transform that lemonade into a money-making opportunity. *How, you ask, do I profit from painful situations in life?*

Wherever you're reading this right now, I want you to sit up a little straighter, because if you can internalize and understand this teaching, your life will never be the same.

> There is a market for your misery, a customer for your crisis,
> and a patron for your pain.

What I mean by that statement is simply this: There are people out there right now who will pull out cash, write checks, or swipe credit cards to pay to learn what you've gone through, and most importantly, how you came out of it. Now let me be very clear: I'm not talking about merchandising someone's misery or about some cheap way of capitalizing on somebody's catastrophe. What I'm saying is that everything you undergo produces a life lesson. And the beautiful part of that is that people *want* to learn how to advance their lives and take themselves to the next level. How do they do that? By teaching other people what they've learned, experienced, and overcome.

Think about this: Every seminar, bootcamp, workshop, coaching program, book, training system, and classroom is filled with people who pay money to learn from "successful people" how they became successful. And a major component of every success story is how that person endured and triumphed over failure, struggle, and adversity. For example:

- Most financially successful leaders have had bankruptcies, credit issues, or money problems somewhere on the road to wealth.

- Real estate tycoons have often botched a number of deals and lost a lot of money before discovering the secret to mastering the market.

- Many of the greatest relationship gurus have been divorced, separated, or been in multiple relationships before becoming better partners.

- Some of the most well-respected people in ministry and the religious community have struggled in their own spiritual growth and development.

My point to you is simple, my friend: *There is no success without adversity.*

There's a market for your misery.

Perhaps one of the greatest examples of this lies in Chris Gardner, the man at the center of the film *The Pursuit of Happyness.* If you saw the movie, you know it was the true story of a man who became a single father, struggled to sell bone density scanners to doctors to try to keep himself and his son off the street, ended up homeless, and got kicked out of motel after motel, having to resort to sleeping in public bathrooms and bathing in sinks before becoming a Wall Street giant and millionaire. It makes us think: If *he* can do it, *I* can certainly do it!

Was there a huge market for Chris Gardner's misery? Yes. So much so that a bestselling book and blockbuster movie were born of it.

There's a customer for your crisis.

Let's assume you had a health emergency, but by the grace of God you were able to overcome it. Perhaps you were on your death bed with obesity and cancer and you discovered natural ways not only to heal yourself, but to lose a significant amount of weight as well. Because there are so many Americans fighting cancer and obesity, writing a book about your experience would likely result in a *New York Times* bestseller. Why? Because there are people who need the same help that you did. And the only way they can learn about your success is by learning about your adversity as well.

There are patrons for your pain.

People are truly interested in learning from you, but only if *you* have learned valuable lessons. Dr. Mike Murdock teaches that there are two ways to get wisdom in life: through mistakes and through mentors. As such, many of us are eager to be mentored through workshops, seminars, books, CDs, DVDs, ebooks, articles, and the like, often hoping to learn from your challenge so we don't have to experience it for ourselves.

So I want you to shift a little bit and stop asking yourself: "Why am I going through this?" And start saying: "Who can reap a reward from this experience that I've had?" If you can teach others how you came out of your difficulty and what you did to turn your life around as a result of it, you can change other people's lives for the better. You have the capacity to package this teaching into a course, program, or system that can help others, but in order to do that, my friend, you have to learn how to shift your paradigm from *My storm is a problem* to *My storm is an opportunity to help someone else and make a profit at the same time.*

Imagine a rainstorm is coming:

One man looks at the sky and says: "Oh my gosh, it's getting ready to rain, what am I going to do?" He then runs and takes shelter inside, never considering anyone but himself.	The other looks up and thinks: "There are thousands of people without umbrellas." So he sets up an umbrella stand on the corner and makes five hundred dollars in an hour.

Clearly one man was shortsighted, while the other realized there was a market for the misery, a customer for the crisis, a patron for the pain. He solved a problem.

My friend, I want you to begin doing something important to aid you in taking those lemons, making some lemonade, and selling it for profit: **Journal your process**. It's vital that you start keeping a written or electronic record of your journey where you write down:

+ your thoughts
+ your pains
+ your lows
+ your highs
+ your breakthroughs
+ your lessons
+ the days you didn't feel like getting out of bed

+ the days you felt disappointed
+ the days you felt rejected
+ the days you felt embarrassed
+ the days you felt on top of the world
+ the days you were mad at God
+ the day you finally realized the lesson life was teaching you

Remember what I told you in chapter one: People are in one of three places—either in a storm, heading toward a storm, or just leaving a storm. So if you're in one right now and you journal and learn from your experience, you can then market your lesson to others, arming them with tools to come through their situation, rebound effectively, and get back in the game of life.

Nothing you've experienced has been a waste of time; everything has a purpose, and all things are working together for your good, even if it's hard to see at present. And you need to understand that if you're going to stage an incredible comeback from life's setbacks, you've got to capture the process in writing. As you do so, ask yourself smart questions, such as:

How can other people benefit from this?

How can I teach what I've been through?

How can I find a group of people through social media, Meetup.com, networking, relationship building, or other resources through which I can offer a seminar/ teaching to help others?

Whether it's family, money, career, health, mind, body, spirit, relationships, or marriage, you have the ability to take the tough lemons that life has dealt you, make some really good, sweet lemonade, and go out and sell it for profit.

When you impact people's lives with your story, your message, and how you've been able to overcome adversity, guess what's going to happen? People will start coming up to you after your workshops and talks, after reading your book or listening to your audio program, and they'll say: "You've changed my life. When you shared that story, when you relayed that lesson, when you told me about that disappointment, it really helped me." And you know what all of that feedback is going to do? It's going to heal you. And you're going to understand why you went through everything you did. You'll realize that it really wasn't about you to begin with, that trouble didn't come *to* you, but was coming *through* you to benefit somebody else.

Delatorro L. McNeal, II

CHAPTER SUMMARY

Though the concept may be new to you, brainstorming a way to profit from your pain is a surefire method of shifting your perspective on the adversity you're experiencing. To that end, I want you to:

- ✦ Begin keeping a journal of your challenge, noting all the emotions you're feeling.

- ✦ Think about who could benefit from your learning.

- ✦ Consider the venue in which you could help others (seminars, books, etc).

- ✦ After the lesson is clear, create an appropriate package you can feasibly deliver that will benefit others.

- ✦ Take pride in knowing you've transformed a negative for yourself into a positive for yourself and others.

Massive Action Plan

Write down your action plan based on what you learned from this chapter.

_____

_____

_____

_____

_____

Go Live!

12

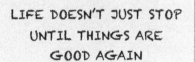

LIFE DOESN'T JUST STOP
UNTIL THINGS ARE
GOOD AGAIN

Somewhere, right now, *someone is smiling* ... Somewhere, right now, *someone is holding a newborn baby* ... Somewhere, right now, *someone is laughing their head off* ...

Somewhere, right now,
someone is enjoying their dream vacation.

∽

Somewhere, right now,
someone is watching their favorite TV show.

∽

Somewhere, right now,
someone is eager to get off a plane to see their loved ones.

Somewhere, right now,

someone is making a deposit into their bank account and they're excited about it.

Somewhere, right now,

someone is enjoying a full body massage.

Somewhere, right now,

someone is making love to their spouse.

Somewhere, right now,

someone is enjoying a nice meal with good friends.

Somewhere, right now,

someone is singing in the shower and sounding really bad and loving it.

Somewhere, right now,

someone is enjoying a stage production.

Somewhere, right now,

someone is walking through the mall and making purchases of things that make them smile.

Somewhere, right now,

someone is tanning under the hot, beautiful sun.

Somewhere, right now,

someone is picking up their kids from school,
happy about the great time their children just had learning.

Somewhere, right now,

someone is having fun texting friends.

Somewhere, right now,

someone is flirting with the person they love and making plans to have a hot date tonight.

∽

Somewhere, right now,

someone is working late to provide for their family.

∽

Somewhere, right now,

someone is enjoying a cruise somewhere in the world.

∽

Somewhere, right now,

someone is writing a book that will become a New York Times bestseller.

∽

Somewhere, right now,

someone is on stage empowering the lives of people from various walks of life.

∽

Somewhere, right now,

someone is praying for their family, their career, their friends, this country, their business, their neighborhood.

∽

Somewhere, right now,

someone is praying for you.

∽

Somewhere, right now,

someone is thinking good thoughts about you.

∽

Somewhere, right now,

someone is wishing you would call them.

∽

Somewhere, right now,

someone is getting ready to go see a brand new blockbuster movie.

Delatorro L. McNeal, II

Somewhere, right now,

someone is exercising and loving the results they're getting.

∽

Somewhere, right now,

someone is learning a new skill, a new language, a new recipe.

∽

Somewhere, right now,

someone is attending a networking function and meeting new people in their community.

∽

Somewhere, right now,

someone is driving past a car accident, thankful they were not involved and saying a prayer for those who were.

∽

Somewhere, right now,

someone is getting married.

∽

Somewhere, right now,

someone is giving birth to a new baby.

∽

Somewhere, right now,

someone is writing in their journal all the great things they want to achieve in their life.

∽

Somewhere, right now,

someone is crafting a vision board, wall, or book of all the things they want to accomplish.

∽

Somewhere, right now,

someone is gaining knowledge and skills at a college or university that will make them a valuable professional when they graduate.

∽

Somewhere, right now,

someone is connecting with friends and family on social media.

Somewhere, right now,

someone is shooting a video they're getting ready to upload to YouTube, and they can't wait to see how many people will watch it.

Somewhere, right now,

someone is making money—a lot of money ... legally.

Somewhere, right now,

someone is buying a new car, boat, truck, motorcycle, or house and they're really excited about it.

Somewhere, right now,

someone is booking a plane ticket to go see someone they care about deeply.

Somewhere, right now,

someone is opening up an acceptance letter to their favorite university.

Somewhere, right now,

someone is cheering for their favorite sports team.

Somewhere, right now,

someone is enjoying an evening of dancing at a club, bar, or hot spot.

Somewhere, right now,

someone is making a difference in the lives of others.

"Well, Del, what's your point?" you may be asking. "You've made a hearty list about *somewhere, right now, someone is doing something.*" My point is very simple, my friend. While you're going through whatever challenge you may be facing, I've got a newsflash for you:

Delatorro L. McNeal, II

> **Life is happening all around you all the time.**

Life doesn't stop just because you're going through a difficult time. So in order to thrive through your storm, you have to learn how to move through it in the most positive way. And once you've taken all the intelligent, strategic action you've learned from this book, you have to do me one favor: **Live, my friend, live**.

Life is happening all around you, and right now I want you to get up and go live it. I want you to go do something awesome, fun, inspiring, or engaging. Interrupt your pattern. Get out of the house, get off the computer, get out of whatever has got you bogged down, and go do something that represents you living life. Let your situation work itself out; better yet, let God work on it while you take a break.

I once heard my mom say this: "Baby, God is up 24/7 so you don't have to be." I love that because let's face it: there's only so much action you can take within your storm. So you've got to do yourself a favor and go out there and live life because it's meant to be lived. This is not a rehearsal, this is it. So, right now, do this for your buddy, Del:

Be that person who is somewhere, right now, reclaiming control of their life and loving every minute of it. My friend, go live!

CHAPTER SUMMARY

When we're embroiled in our own problems, we often forget that life is happening outside of our troubled world. But it is. And just because you're experiencing a trial doesn't mean you're supposed to be focused on it at all times, that you're not allowed to take a break from it and enjoy life in spite of the difficulty you're going through. In fact, I urge you to embrace something fun or relaxing, *especially* when you're overwhelmed with challenge. My friend, it doesn't have to cost a thing if money's your issue:

+ Play a sport
+ Take a walk in the park
+ Play music and sing out loud

+ Watch a DVD at home
+ Meditate
+ Hang out in a bookstore or library

And if you have some cash to play with, go out and:

+ Go to a play or concert
+ Go shopping
+ Have a meal in a nice restaurant

+ See a movie
+ Go bowling with friends
+ Have fun at an amusement park

Massive Action Plan

Write down your action plan based on what you learned from this chapter.

_____

_____

_____

_____

Delatorro L. McNeal, II

Afterword

Congratulations, my friend! You made it. You not only finished this book, but you learned a process I know has permanently shifted the way you approach the storms of your past, present, and even your future.

In the introduction, I gave you a new equation to help you process whatever comes into your life more positively.

$$E + R = O$$

Event + Response = Outcome

Then, I challenged you to allow this book to change the *meaning* you associate to the storms you experience in life. In the direct, in-your-face content that followed, I taught you to specifically address the adversity and obstacles you face in all aspects of your life. If you internalized all the ways to do that, you should now have a completely new mental and emotional operating system with which to process the storms that come into your life and the lives of those you know, love, and care about.

I promised to teach you 12 Profound Lessons, so let's review them to keep them fresh in your mind.

In **Chapter 1**, I taught you the importance of being prepared for adversity long before it ever comes knocking on your door. Remember: We are in one of three places at any given point—in a storm, just left a storm, or heading toward a storm.

In **Chapter 2**, I shared with you seven lessons from Failure 101, the course you've been learning all your life but never took in school. These lessons will help you process your storms not as failures, but as feedback.

In **Chapter 3**, I actually took you with me, into the storm itself, and showed you how to exist within it, endure, focus your mind on the outcome, and ride through it powerfully.

In **Chapter 4**, I helped you realize that in life you don't either Win or Lose, you actually Win or Learn. So as long as you keep learning from what you go through in life, you always WIN.

In **Chapter 5**, I helped you see that you are stronger than you realize, and sometimes life's storms come to bring that greater and stronger person out of you that would have never come out otherwise.

In **Chapter 6**, I taught you how to Thrive Through the Loss of a loved one and how to allow yourself to grieve. I also offered ways you can begin the process of healing and moving forward in honor of the person you lost.

In **Chapter 7**, I challenged you to Know Your Value and to never allow what happens to you to negatively impact your perception of yourself and your own self-worth.

In **Chapter 8**, I replaced those negative questions—those we all tend to ask ourselves during tough times—with 10 better questions that will empower you to live life at a new level and learn from every experience you have.

In **Chapter 9**, I put you in the seat of the bus driver and reminded you to Keep Driving the Bus, allowing people to get on and off your bus in life while you keep the final destination in mind and enjoy the journey.

In **Chapter 10**, I inspired you to take your power back by getting on the offensive rather than the defensive and taking a more proactive role in your comeback. You are no more the victim; you are now the victor!

In **Chapter 11**, I gave you money-making ideas that will help you take the lemons that life hands you, make some good old-fashioned lemonade, and go out there and sell it for profit. Remember: There's a market for your misery and a customer for your crisis.

In **Chapter 12**, I reminded you that life doesn't stop just because you're going through a difficult season in your life. Life moves on and so should you. So go out there and live life to the fullest right in the middle of your difficult time, because somewhere, right now, someone is doing something awesome with their life … why not you?

So, my friend, I've done my job. I kept my promise to teach you 12 Profound Lessons for Thriving Through Your Storms. Now, the rest of the work is truly on you to implement all I've taught you so you can truly *grow* through anything you *go* through in life.

It is my sincere hope and prayer that you have been challenged, stretched, equipped, inspired, motivated, supported, and educated during our time together, and all I ask now is that you take what I've taught you, apply it to your life, and then share this message with others by:

+ Encouraging friends to buy a copy of this book.
+ Posting about this book and its impact on social media.
+ Forming study groups and book clubs around this book.
+ Inviting me to come to your company, organization, professional association, community group, church, college, or business to talk about this book.
+ Purchasing this book in bulk for groups of individuals you know need it, but maybe can't afford it.
+ Joining our online community at: www.ThrivingThroughYourStorms.com so we can keep you encouraged and you can inspire others with your comeback story.

I believe that as soon as you have been blessed to learn something amazing, you immediately have an obligation to teach it to others. Let's partner together to help people all over the world Thrive!

Your Platinum Partner,

Delatorro L. McNeal, II, MS, CSP

About the Author

Delatorro McNeal II, MS, CSP is an internationally renowned peak performance expert, leadership keynote speaker, bestselling author, and television host. His expertise has been featured on FOX, NBC, ABC, TBN, OWN, and Oxygen, and he has delivered over 3000 paid presentations to Fortune 100 corporations, professional associations, sales/leadership conferences, colleges and universities, and churches all over the world. As the Chairman and CEO of Platinum Performance Global, LLC, he helps individuals and organizations GROW to the next level.

Delatorro is also a Certified Speaking Professional, which places him in the top 7% of paid professional speakers worldwide who are members of the National Speakers Association and The Global Speakers Federation. Known for his hard-hitting, no-nonsense success psychology that inspires millions to take massive strategic action to create the lives of their dreams, Delatorro is also the founder of The Full Throttle Experience: 3-Day LIVE Leaderpreneurship Conference. To learn more, visit:

www.FullThrottleExperience.com.

Connect with Delatorro online by searching "Delatorro" on:

www.Delatorro.com
www.ThrivingThroughYourStorms.com
www.FullThrottleExperience.com
www.CrushUniversity.com
www.CaughtBetweenADreamAndAJob.com

Office: (813) 963-5356
Email: Delatorro@gmail.com

Platinum Performance Global, LLC
13194 US HWY 301 S
Suite #211
Riverview, FL 33578

Made in the USA
Coppell, TX
09 November 2024

39864100R00085